proclamation 2

Aids for Interpreting the Lessons of the Church Year

holy week

Richard J. Clifford
and
Hays H. Rockwell

series c

editors: Elizabeth Achtemeier · Gerhard Krodel · Charles P. Price

FORTRESS PRESS PHILADELPHIA

Second printing 1982

Library of Congress Cataloging In Publication Data (Revised)

Main entry under title:

Proclamation 2.

Consists of 24 volumes in 3 series designated A, B, and C which correspond to the cycles of the three year lectionary plus 4 volumes covering the lesser festivals. Each series contains 8 basic volumes with the following titles: Advent-Christmas, Epiphany, Lent, Holy Week, Easter, Pentecost 1, Pentecost 2, and Pentecost 3.

CONTENTS: [etc.]—Series C: [1] Fuller, R. H. Advent-Christmas. [2] Pervo, R. I. and Carl III, W. J. Epiphany.—Thulin, R. L. et al. The lesser festivals. 4 v.

1. Bible—Homiletical use. 2. Bible—Liturgical lessons, English.

[BS534.5.p76] 251 79-7377

ISBN 0-8006-4079-9 (ser. C, v. 1)

332A83 Printed in the United States of America 1-4088

Contents

Editor's Foreword

In the celebration of Holy Week, the biblical drama of the salvation of the world is now moving rapidly toward its climax. That which was hidden in two thousand years of history is now soon to be revealed: God's lordship over all the earth, to which every knee shall bow. At the center of the drama are the suffering and glorification of Jesus Christ. Thus the lessons of the Sunday of the Passion (Palm Sunday) tell the story of his suffering and promise his exaltation to glory. The lessons of each day of the week spell out the significance of these events.

Two traditions merge on the Sunday before Easter: the fourth-century Jerusalem custom of commemorating the triumphal entry in a procession of palms, and the fifth-century Western commemoration of the day as the beginning of the Lord's final passion. It was the latter which passed into the Reformation, but in the present lectionary, the two have been almost combined: the story of the passion is read, but the joyful mood of the triumphal entry is preserved by the OT and Epistle lessons.

Maundy Thursday's name is taken from the Latin, *mandatum* = "commandment," remembering Jesus' words "A new commandment I give to you . . ." at the washing of the disciples' feet. The ceremony of foot washing was widely practiced in the Middle Ages and in Reformation England, but it is the eucharistic imitation of the Last Supper which predominates in practice. In the custom of the fourth-century Jerusalem church, this was followed by a visit to Gethsemane after midnight.

In the primitive church, Good Friday and Holy Saturday were originally simply fast days in preparation for baptism and participation in the Easter Eucharist. It was, again, the fourth-century Jerusalem church which introduced the three-hour Friday service of reading, hymns, and preaching so often found today. The Jerusalem service took place at the actual site of Golgotha, followed by a visit to the Holy Sepulcher in the evening.

The rites of Holy Saturday all originally belonged to Easter Eve, with its midnight mass. The day then became a time of baptism and confirmation, looking forward to the first Communion at the Easter mass.

The earliest allusions to marking Holy Week as a whole are found in the *Apostolic Constitutions* of the last half of the third century A.D., where abstinence from wine and meat is enjoined, along with an absolute fast on Friday and Saturday.

Richard J. Clifford, the exegete for this volume, is an associate professor at Weston School of Theology and a visiting lecturer at Harvard. He received his Ph.D. from Harvard, and is the General Editor of the *Catholic Biblical Quarterly,* as well as the author of *The Cosmic Mountain in Canaan and in the Old Testament* and of numerous scholarly articles.

The Reverend Hays H. Rockwell, the homiletician, has been rector of St. James' Church in New York City since 1976. Educated at Brown University and the Episcopal Divinity School in Massachusetts, he has served as chaplain at several schools and colleges, and on numerous boards and agencies of the Protestant Episcopal Church. He holds an honorary D.D. degree from Kenyon College.

Richmond, Va. ELIZABETH ACHTEMEIER

Sunday of the Passion
Palm Sunday

Lutheran	Roman Catholic	Episcopal	Pres/UCC/Chr	Meth/COCU
Deut. 32:36–39	Isa. 50:4–7	Isa. 45:21–25 or Isa. 52:13—53:12	Isa. 59:14–20	Deut. 32:36–39
Phil. 2:5–11	Phil. 2:6–11	Phil. 2:5–11	1 Tim. 1:12–17	Phil. 2:5–11
Luke 22:1—23:56 or Luke 23:1–49	Luke 22:14—23:56 or Luke 23:1–49	Luke (22:39–71) 23:1–49 (50-56)	Luke 19:28–40	Luke 22:1—23:56

EXEGESIS

First Lesson: Isa. 45:21–25. This lesson seems to have been selected because v. 23, "To me every knee shall bow, every tongue shall swear," is reused in the second reading, Phil. 2:10–11. Both lessons deal with the manifestation of the hidden glory of God which leads to universal confession. The readings therefore complement admirably the Lucan passion account of glory deliberately laid aside.

All the OT readings in Holy Week C except two are from Second Isaiah. His proper name is not known; Second Isaiah is the name given him by modern scholars. He lived in the period of the exile of the Jews in Babylon (587–539 B.C.), over five hundred miles as the crow flies from the holy city of Jerusalem, but in reality much longer when we take into consideration the ordinary route and means of transportation. He preached in the latter half of the Exile, probably from the 550s, since he often speaks of Cyrus the Persian who came to international prominence only from this time. The religious crisis addressed by the prophet was directly the result of the national collapse before the armies of Babylon. The temple in Jerusalem was destroyed and the leading citizens were deported to Babylon. To understand the depth of the crisis we must keep in mind ancient Near Eastern religious thought. The god or gods who were experienced on earth as most powerful in critical times such as major battles were thought to be most powerful in the heavens, the world of the gods. According to this ingrained way of thinking which influenced Jew and Babylonian alike, Bel-Marduk and the other chief deities of Babylon had defeated Yahweh the god of the Jews, and had thus risen to preeminence in heaven and on earth. Yahweh had been able to protect neither his people Israel from death and deportation nor his temple shrine from destruction. Bel-Marduk and the Babylonian pantheon had demonstrated their power. People recognized their supremacy and celebrated it liturgically in magnificent processions of the victorious god's statue to his temple. For exiled Jews to see with their own eyes splendid celebrations of the power of Bel-Marduk, and to experience the silence of their own god, must have been devastating to their sense of themselves as Yahweh's people. A silent or hidden god was no god at all. A god who does not act in the world has no power, does not exist. His people cannot celebrate his "glory," or earthly manifestation of his supremacy.

In preaching good news to the exiles, Second Isaiah had to interpret the true meaning of world history and the power of the other gods. Yahweh's silence in the years of exile had to be explained as due not to defeat but to his will to punish Israel for earlier covenant breach. But now is the time of forgiveness (Isa. 40:1–2) and for displaying his glory, that is, for showing visibly on earth the power which he has in heaven, the world of the gods.

To portray the cosmic scope of the message, the prophet situates the speech of God in a legal trial of the nations and their gods. In the ancient world the god (represented by his image) and the nation were intimately associated, so that the prosperity of the people reflected the power of the deity. Similar trial scenes are found in 41:1–5, 21–29; 43:8–13; and 44:6–8. In this genre, Yahweh as judge directs questions against the nations and their gods to show that he is master of both the human and divine world.

The correct unit here is 45:20–25, not 21–25 as the lectionary has it. The nations and the gods they carry, their images, are summoned to a trial (v. 20) and then are subjected to relentless cross-examination. The phrase "survivors of the nations" refers in all probability to those national groups that were beginning to be displaced by the conquests of Cyrus the Persian, who was at the time systematically conquering the Babylonian Empire. Second Isaiah elsewhere (44:24—45:13, esp. 44:28; 45:1-4, 13) makes it clear that Yahweh is behind Cyrus, who is breaking up the rule of Babylon (and of course the rule of Babylon's gods). The questions "Who told this aforetime? Who foretold it of old?" ask the national gods which of them had spoken words which made it possible for Cyrus to conquer as a divine instrument. Second Isaiah appears to refer here to ancient Israelite traditions which showed the tyrant as Yahweh's unwitting instrument, for example Pharaoh in Exodus 1—15 and the Assyrian king in Isa. 10:5-15 + 14:24-27. Yahweh alone, and not the other gods, has shown in the past the power to bring all earthly rulers ultimately to do his will. After the impotent silence of the nations and gods (v. 21), Yahweh answers that he alone has the power; he is God. Vv. 20-21 have shown in court that the nations' gods have had nothing to do with the turn in world history caused by Cyrus' victories. Yahweh who is behind Cyrus is the only powerful Deity. Vv. 22-24 then call all the nations to turn to this single powerful God and find success (v. 22). RSV "find salvation" is perhaps too specific. While the nations are invited to see the triumph of Yahweh, they do not take part in salvation in the same way as the Israelites do. The one God's word declares that he alone has divine power and that it is now visible to all (vv. 22-23). Vv. 24-25 say that only through Yahweh's power has Israel found victory (for RSV "righteousness") and strength, and their offspring vindication and glory. In other words, the nation that seemed dead because of the impotence of its god now lives unto succeeding generations.

The genre that the prophet has chosen for his message—the public trial of the nations—shows us that Yahweh's freeing of his people is a matter for the whole world to acknowledge. It is a refutation of all other powers which people have adored. It invites those left holding lifeless idols in their hands to bow down before the mighty Lord who has chosen to save his people Israel.

Second Lesson: Phil. 2:5-11. There is virtual agreement today among exegetes that the famous christological hymn of vv. 6-11 was not written by Paul (except for the addition of "even death on a cross" of v. 8) but adapted by him as part of a long instruction to the community (1:27—2:18). In the exhortation Paul wishes to inculcate in his readers steadfastness, harmony, humility, and obedient unselfishness. The hymn illustrates humility. The non-Pauline character of the hymn is shown by its passing directly from cross to exaltation without mention of the resurrection and by its un-Pauline vocabulary, for example "to empty oneself," "form of God," "being equal to God," "something to be used for one's own advantage." The hymn has been variously analyzed. E. Lohmeyer sees it as two matching panels, vv. 6–8 and 9–11, each of which consists of three strophes, vv. 6, 7, 8 and vv. 9, 10, 11. J. Jeremias has more recently proposed three stanzas: (1) 6–7a (ending with the phrase "taking the form of a slave"); (2) 7b–8; (3) 9–11. Both outlines are heuristically valuable. Whatever one's poetic analysis, it is clear that the liturgical poem celebrates Christ's astonishing passage from heavenly glory to earthly bondage and death, and then from lowliness to a glory granted by the Father that will be seen and recognized by all peoples. V. 6 portrays the heavenly Christ exercising the free choice of laying aside the "form of God," that is, the dazzling brilliance that accompanied the Deity in earthly manifestations. In the OT it is called the glory of the Lord. He chose not to treat his equality with God as something to be used to his own advantage. He rather emptied himself of that outward glory which was his right and became man, taking on the outward appearance of a slave (v. 7). In the biblical view, it is a characteristic of man to be obedient. And that is what Christ does. God the Father's response to Christ divesting himself of glory is to "super-exalt" him above all in heaven and earth, and to display him with his proper glory so that all nations may see and acknowledge his sovereignty. The hymn quotes the passage from Second Isaiah discussed under the First Lesson. Christ who has given up his glory for the sake of humankind by being powerless is now able to receive it back from the Father as a gift, and in a way that can be recognized by all.

Paul does not quote this hymn merely to embroider the letter. He wishes to make the Philippian community more solidly grounded in Christ. V. 5, "Have this mind among you which you have in Christ Jesus," can mean of course that the community members in imitation of Christ are to be humble and not to seek their own needs first

(v. 3). The Greek can also be translated, "Have for one another that attitude which you also have in Christ Jesus," meaning that the community should let the vital union which they have with Christ appear in their loving and self-effacing relationships with each other. It is not only the example of Christ which should compel. They are also linked in some fashion to the drama of the self-donating Christ so that they can count on the Father's merciful crowning of their humble service of each other. Thus Paul demonstrates his ability to put his beloved community in fruitful contact with the self-abasing and trusting Christ whom they hymn.

Gospel: Luke 22:1—23:56. At first glance the accounts of the passion in the three synoptic Gospels and even in John appear remarkably alike. The early standardization of the passion in the gospel tradition reflects the need of the Christian community, felt even before the composition of Mark in the 60s A.D., to explain the scandal of the disgraceful death of their Messiah. His suffering and death was not a sign of his rejection by God—the conventional interpretation of a violent and premature death—but was in accord with the Scriptures (the OT) and hence intended by God. Within the traditional passion scheme, each evangelist managed to underline his favorite themes. In the interest of economy of space, it seems best to point out in Luke's long account only those important themes which appear also in the lessons from Second Isaiah and Philippians: the divine glory contained in a hidden way in God's servant is revealed to the world.

More so than Mark and Matthew, Luke makes the last supper central to his Gospel. As is explained in more detail under Maundy Thursday, Luke alone mentions one of the three cups of wine which are part of the Passover meal, and twice stresses that the entire meal points forward to fulfillment in the kingdom of God (22:15–18). The Messiah was expected to appear at the Passover, according to popular belief, in order to inaugurate the kingdom of God.

In other passages, especially Luke 17:21, Jesus had announced the kingdom as present in the midst of his hearers. In his total work, Luke-Acts, the evangelist demonstrates that the coming of God's kingdom in Jesus is a gradual process, successively appearing in the OT, in Jesus himself in a hidden way, in the church as the apostles find themselves empowered to do what Jesus did, and definitively in the final age. Thus Jesus does afresh the ancient wonders described in the Scriptures, while his own work of healing and preaching foreshadows and validates the apostles' mighty works in Acts. And all of these works and wonders point forward to their final fulfillment in the last age.

The last supper in Luke shares in this backward and forward movement. The covenant meal of Exodus 24 at which the covenant between God and Moses was ratified lives again in Luke's supper scene. The banquet also has a proleptic, or anticipatory, function. It is indeed the meal in which the fruits of Jesus' self-offering are shared with his disciples, but it is also the anticipation of the last age when the dispersed people will be gathered together. Only Luke of the synoptics speaks of the new covenant here (22:20; RSV marg.), alluding to Jer. 31:31–34 when Israel will be gathered for a new covenant. The meal not only ratifies the new covenant. It is also in anticipation the final banquet inaugurating the new unity won by Christ. He it is who presides over the gathered Israel.

The glory of the banquet in which all sit peaceably together around their Lord is hidden, as the next scene shows (22:24–27). Luke is careful to place this scene at the banquet. The disciples must learn how to exercise the power granted to them in the kingdom—not in the manner of the world but humbly after Christ's example. Their authority as rulers is real though hidden. Luke puts Peter's denial at the supper (22:31–34) rather than on the way to the garden as Mark does, probably in order to explain further the theme of hidden rulership begun in vv. 24–30.

If the account of the supper is resumptive and anticipatory of the rule of God over the world, several further Lucan incidents show that the passion is regarded as a great trial scene in which the suffering Jesus is publicly vindicated as righteous. The new age, it was commonly believed, would be introduced by a great trial in which the children of light and the children of darkness would be in conflict. In some versions of the struggle heavenly beings and humans are depicted as fighting side by side. In 22:42–44, one of these heavenly figures comforts Jesus in the hour of trial. (There is some uncertainty in the reading.) Herod and Pilate, rulers of this world, join forces to condemn the righteous one (23:6–16). The women of Jerusalem are urged to mourn over the coming judgment consequent upon the rejection of the righteous one (23:27–31). In the hour of judgment repentant sinners are able to enter paradise (23:39–43). At the end the centurion declares that the one who died at the hands of sinners is vindicated and exalted before the wicked generation as a proof of God's upholding his cause. "Certainly this man was innocent" (23:47), declares the centurion, an echo of the vindication of the righteous sufferer in the Psalms of lament, of such trial scenes as Daniel 3, 6, and the Wisd. of Sol. 1:16—5:23. The glory of God comes into public visibility by the faithfulness of the servant.

HOMILETICAL INTERPRETATION

Palm Sunday worship is dominated by the long and potent Gospel lesson. It is Luke's version of the passion story, and the whole of it—two chapters—is designated to be read and listened to by Palm Sunday's gathered congregations. Sometimes the reading is done by a number of people, taking parts, so that the congregation is in a way drawn into the action surrounding the last days and hours of persecution and suffering. However it is read, the Gospel lesson for this day means to put at the head of the week the whole painful, hope-filled story of the days that lead to Easter. To live with that story, and all of its consequences and subsequences in human history, is at the heart of what it means for preacher and people to "keep" Holy Week.

It is of course a story with a past, and its meaning can only be found when that past is seriously addressed. One means to that task is in addressing the verses that constitute the First Lesson for Palm Sunday.

First Lesson: Isa. 45:21–25. The great songs of Second Isaiah influence the gospel stories and the teaching of Jesus in countless ways and in numerous places. They are songs of hope and expectation. At the same time they come out of a period in Israel's precarious history which was marked by uncertainty and jeopardy. They are songs that proclaim hope, but they were first sung within a context of threatening and unpredictable events, events over which a captive Israel had no control. To speak of hope in the way that Second Isaiah spoke of it is precisely *not* to evade history. There is in this poetry no attempt to escape into the false safety of fantasy and illusion. There is instead a bold willingness to confront events in all of their harshness, and *then* to speak hopefully. Hope of that kind is born of the certainty that the one who is finally in charge of events, of all history, is the gracious and righteous God, the one who is victorious and able to save (Isa. 45:22). That *that* one is a participant in the world's life means that although there may be very much in the way of uncertainty all around us, the outcome is secure.

What the striking changes of history reveal most clearly is the transiency of human power and authority. The Babylonian Empire was a great and mighty thing to behold, but it fell like a helpless child before Cyrus and the armies of Persia. Not their politics, not their military strength, not even their splendidly colorful religion could save the Babylonians. So it was that Persia and her descendant kingdoms yielded to Alexander the Great, and so it has always been and evermore shall be In all of that, and in the striking changes that occur in the tiny histories that are our lives, the Bible's word is of hope. The Bible speaks of a God of hope whose promise is not of an illusory kingdom where there is eternal safety from events. The God of hope of whom the Bible speaks, of whom Isaiah sings, is the one in whom "righteousness" and "strength" are met in the here and now of our lives.

The story that occupies the community of Christians in Holy Week speaks of that meeting of righteousness and strength by speaking of a weak and apparently helpless country preacher, a victim of misunderstanding and fear, the pushover loser in a minor power struggle. The claim that story makes, like the claim of the distant and anonymous Second Isaiah, is that we should look for the present God, not by worshiping the triumphs of men but by searching with care the heart of the world's defeat.

Second Lesson: Phil. 2:5–11. Is there any more sublime hymn of our faith than this great fragment from a letter to the Philippians? Its source is in the earliest life of the Christian community (see exegesis) so that in it we hear not an echo but a clear, original song of faith and praise from the first church.

What song does our latter-day church sing? What *ought* we to be singing on the spring morning that is also Palm Sunday? There are temptations of very many kinds. Some would have us singing things soft and soothing, music meant to turn the dusty road into the garden path. Some call the modern church to play martial songs, songs that summon the faithful to this battlement or that one. There are those of sophisticated taste who yearn for a church in which only the highest aesthetic standard is sought, by the most gifted musicians.

Nor are all of these claims necessarily beside the gospel's point. The modern church, the church in every age, *is* in fact called to provide comfort by what it says and sings and does. The church *is* meant to stir up hearts for the struggle against the dark forces of the world's life. And the church is a company of men and women charged with celebrating its Lord in the "beauty of holiness."

Yet there is a deep sense in which all of these claims, pertinent as they may be to the proclamation, speak of penultimate things, of derivative responsibilities. The primary responsibility of the faithful church is to set forth, by what it says and sings and does, the triumphant hymn of Philippians 2. For it is the church's main work to proclaim what God has done, and these brief verses do precisely that. The God for whom the church exists is the one whose Son "humbled himself" by taking on human form, who came willy-nilly into the mortal midst. Nor was he merely in disguise, playing the tricks which any respectable god might play as a kind of divine distraction. He invested his whole self, risking glory and honor and dominion and power to the frailty of flesh and blood. To proclaim what God has done is to join Paul in sending the meaning of this hymn to whatever part of the world to which we ourselves are sent to minister. To speak of what God has done in Christ, of this act of extravagant selflessness is, of course, to speak of the essential way that God is. It is to say, of all extraordinary things, that God is eminently *available* in Christ, that having once given over his life to the particular flesh and blood of Jesus of Nazareth, he is forevermore near at hand.

But it is to speak of something else as well. It is to speak of the way God is and to speak also of the way *we* are meant to be. Paul includes this hymn in order that his Philippian listeners may order their relationships to one another after the manner of God's willingness toward them. To proclaim what God has done in Christ is to be bidden to a life in which the primary categories are not "self-fulfillment" and "self-understanding." For the principal call of the Philippians hymn, and of the whole gospel, is a call to selflessness, even to that extravagant selflessness by which God showed himself in Christ Jesus.

That selflessness is our best and truest music at the outset of this Holy Week.

> Such music in its turn becomes the trope
> Or figure of that holy amity
> Which is our only hope.
>
> Anthony Hecht*

Gospel: Luke 22:1—23:56. Here is the week's whole story, the gospel's long word to us. It is an astonishing combination of the sordid and the holy. It is the Palm Sunday Gospel, but at least in this lectionary we are given no palms, no parades, no ambiguous "hosannas." We are given instead a story of betrayal and persecution that ends in bloody death. It is the story which, in differing forms and versions, will occupy the church for all of the week ahead.

To have it all read out at once, even over the commotion of squirming children and the impatient coughs of the disinterested, may bring home to us that we are meant to fix minds and hearts on *this* story and no other. There are some seductive forces at work to draw us away from the passion story. They tempt us, for instance, to look instead upon the stories of our own sufferings, to look away from the cross in order to concentrate upon *our* humiliations. But the story of our grief is not the story for this week. The story for this week is the story of the suffering and humiliation of Christ. In the version of it in the Fourth Gospel Pilate is made to say of Jesus, "Behold the man." That is what we are meant to say. Not

*Anthony Hecht, "Gladness of the Best," in *Millions of Strange Shadows* (New York: Atheneum Publishers, 1977).

"Behold *my* grievances, the dread and the tragedy that have broken into my life since the last Holy Week." Not "Behold my private distress that I am not successful enough or rich enough or healthy enough or loved enough." Not even "Behold the plight of our city and the precariousness of our nation, and of the whole warring planet." None of that, not at least in this week. In this week we are called, first of all by the Palm Sunday Gospel lesson, to behold the Man.

If there is a hazard of subjectivity on the one hand as we approach the Holy Week story, then on the other hand there is the danger that we may reduce it to a kind of melodrama. When that happens the principal figures become stock characters, shallow prototypes of one or another obvious human trait. They become one-dimensional, predictable. Their actions are the issue of inevitability. To treat the Holy Week events in that way is to remain distant from them, as though they were going on under a faraway proscenium arch: something to be viewed with alarm, perhaps, but surely with detached alarm. Sometimes the so-called Passion Plays have that result, rendering cosmic drama—in all of its density and subtlety—as though it were conventional theater, something one pays for and looks at and walks away from, back into "real" life.

But we are not meant to remain outside the Holy Week events at all. We are meant to be drawn into them so that we become part of their saving action. To be drawn into the story is the purpose and meaning of the worship of the church between Palm Sunday and Easter Day. Looked at in one way, it is the purpose and meaning of the whole of the Christian life: to take hold upon, and be taken hold upon *by,* the story of the sacrificial love of God.

Of central significance to the drama is the meal. (See exegesis.) It is given to us just so that we may be drawn by it into the action of the week. Of course it is the heavenly banquet brought down, the sign of the presence in our midst of the Messiah of God. Yet when you hear of it, among the commonplace actions of embittered and disloyal friends, and the petty cowardice of second-rate politicians, and the bullying of the soldiers, it suddenly becomes the sign to us also of a holy risk, the risk of the One who so loves us that, in the words of the ancient prayer, he was "contented to be betrayed."

Monday in Holy Week

Lutheran	Roman Catholic	Episcopal	Pres/UCC/Chr	Meth/COCU
Isa. 42:1-9	Isa. 42:1-7	Isa. 42:1-9	Isa. 50:4-10	Isa. 42:1-9
Heb. 9:11-15		Heb. 11:39—12:3	Heb. 9:11-15	Heb. 9:11-15
John 12:1-11	John 12:1-11	John 12:1-11 or Mark 14:3-9	Luke 19:41-48	John 12:1-11

EXEGESIS

The readings that have been selected for Monday are less unified than other days' readings. They introduce books or sections of books that will be used again later in the week: John, Hebrews, the so-called servant songs in Second Isaiah (42:1-4 on Monday; 49:1-6 on Tuesday; 50:4-11 on Wednesday; 52:13—53:12, which can be read in each lectionary at some point in Holy Week C but is not treated in this book). Focusing on a few books in Holy Week gives preacher and hearer alike the opportunity to find their way in a limited terrain. The lessons today deal with the service of the chosen one and the life-giving consequences for the people of that costly act of service.

First Lesson: Isa. 42:1-9. Isa. 42:1-4, along with 49:1-6; 50:4-11; and 52:13—53:12, were isolated as poems separate from the rest of Second Isaiah by the influential German commentator Bernhard Duhm in 1892. Once isolated from their context in the book, the servant songs were subjected to minute analysis often with a view to later NT themes. Within recent years there has been a laudable reintegration of the poems within the whole book, chaps. 40—55, and useful comparisons with other passages in the other chapters which use similar vocabulary have been made. Many scholars today recognize the servant in Second Isaiah as a figure depicted in language taken from Israel's earlier traditions regarding prophet and king. Old prophetic and royal language was free to be used in a new way during the Exile because the "normal" or pre-exilic role of king and prophet had undergone radical change. The identity of the servant is controverted still, but he seems to be both an individual and a corporate figure. Fluidity between individual and group was well-known among the Israelites: the patriarch Jacob is called Israel because in him and in his story the whole people is somehow included. Moses and Jeremiah offer further illustrations of the idea. Moses was so closely identified with the people that his own obedience was instrumental in God's sparing the rebellious people in the wilderness. Conversely the people's disobedience prevented his entering the Holy Land. Jeremiah, described with Mosaic traits in his call (cf. Jer. 1:6 and Exod. 4:10), was also so identified with the people that he had to suffer in their refusal to hear the divine word he preached. The servant too is an individual described with resonances of older heroes of the tradition, particularly Moses and Jeremiah, and similarly he is bound in with the life of the people. He is primarily the individual prophet himself, whom we call Second Isaiah. Yet the servant includes all who stand with the prophet in obedience to God's new call.

The new call is the call to return home to Zion in a new exodus-creation and to let themselves be planted anew around the holy shrine. In the first exodus, God overcame the oppressive forces in an act of redemption and creation and led his people to the holy land (Exod. 15:1–18). In the Exile he has again overcome forces that hold the people in thralldom and wishes to lead them back to his holy land. However, many exiles did not want to return to their land. They had settled down and were comfortable where they were. But true Israel must return to their God-given land in procession, which will prove to the world that their God lives and is supremely powerful. True Israel thus represented primarily by the prophet himself will return to the ancient holy land. Like Moses he will bring about the march homeward and like Moses know rejection. The processional journey homeward will be that obediential act that will display God's glory and assure a future to all Israel.

Isa. 42:1–4 seems to be the conclusion of a long poem, 41:1—42:4. The long poem, in two matching sections (41:1–20 and 41:21—42:4), shows the Lord summoning the nations and their gods to answer the question, what god is behind the military success of Cyrus the Persian king (see Sunday's exegesis)? The question is of capital importance because if Yahweh is that God, it proves to the world that he is still powerful and alone controls the destiny of nations and peoples. The gods and their nations cannot respond, as in Sunday's pericope from Second Isaiah. The Lord then turns to Israel (42:1), pointing out that Israel's existence as a people who march to their land is proof of their God's power. Israel obediently making the new exodus then is the servant par excellence, making the glory of their God known throughout the world. Loving language used of the servants of old, the prophets and kings, is now applied to the faithful (v. 1). In returning they display the justice of God's case to all (v. 4). There is no need to speak (v. 2); their presence is enough. V. 3 is obscure because there are no good ancient Near Eastern parallels but may mean that the proclamation will be done by a lowly and militarily powerless people. The servant then in these verses designates Israel brought near to the strengthening presence of God for the purpose of displaying his justice by their obedience.

Vv. 5–9 are a second speech of God to his people with further words of consolation. In a series of participles like those used in the hymns of the Psalter to celebrate deeds of creation and redemption, Yahweh is praised as the creator of heaven and earth and as the maker of humankind (v. 5). The giving of breath and spirit recalls the making of the man in the Garden of Eden (Gen. 2:7) and the reconstituting of Israel in the prophecy of Ezekiel to the dry bones (Ezek. 37:9–10). God tells the reconstituted people he has taken them by the hand to protect them and has made them "a covenant to the people, a light to the nations." The first phrase is somewhat obscure, but the second member of the parallel, "a light to the nations," is fortunately clear. Israel's choice means illumination and freedom for the nations. The phrases of vv. 6b–7 are in approximate parallelism and appear to mean that Israel's revitalization as a people benefits the nations. They are freed from the domination of the no-gods who cannot save. V. 8 seems to echo the dethroning of the other gods by its insistence that Yahweh gives his glory to no other god or image. In v. 9 Yahweh declares that the earlier saving events of the first creation-exodus set in motion by the preaching of the word have already come to pass and that a new creation-exodus is being proclaimed. The words that proclaim them are not mere predictions. The words cause the deed. Israel is hearing from its

God those words which actually are creating it as a new people able to march back to its land and live life anew before its God.

Second Lesson: Heb. 9:11–15. The Epistle to the Hebrews is more accurately characterized as a "word of exhortation" (13:22 and cf. Acts 13:15). It belongs to the early Christian genre of *paraenesis,* "exhortation," calling Christians to renewal of allegiance to Jesus Christ as the sole mediator of their salvation. Though closer to Paul's writings than to other NT compositions, it was not written by Paul. Unique in the NT in style, language, and Christology, the work is the product of an anonymous Christian writing ca. A.D. 80–90. The Christians addressed are linked to the Hebrews of old wandering in the desert in search of God's "rest." The period of the desert wanderings, along with the sacred institutions of those times such as the tabernacle, is looked upon by the author as a type of the new realities of the last age introduced by Christ. Christians are on a journey toward heavenly rest.

Today's passage is taken from a longer section, 8:1—10:31, which describes the sacrifices in the heavenly tabernacle or sacred tent. The argument rests upon assumptions which are foreign to a Western view of reality. In the view of Hebrews, the real, or divine, world is made available to people living on earth in certain institutions which reproduce the form of the heavenly reality. Because these institutions imitate the form of the heavenly archetype, they bring that reality to earth. People can touch the sphere of God's gracious acceptance and favor through the earthly copies of the heavenly reality. One important institution is the ancient tabernacle or tent of the Israelites in the desert period as they wandered toward their "rest," possession of the holy land. The desert tabernacle, predecessor of the Jerusalem temple built later under Solomon, consisted of two contiguous tents, each entered through a curtain. Daily ritual offering was done of course in the open court in front of the tents and not within the tent itself. But once a year on the Day of Atonement (see Leviticus 16), the high priest entered the inner tent, the Holy of Holies (Hebrew idiom for the most holy place). Here were kept the sacred symbols: the chest or ark containing the tablets of the covenant, the so-called mercy seat, or elaborate cover of the ark at each end of which was the cherub (image of a lionlike animal). This was considered the earthly throne of God.* In this hallowed place which, because it is the copy of the heavenly reality, "participates" in the very holiness of God, the priest sprinkles the blood of a bull in atonement for sin.

For the author of Hebrews, the desert tabernacle was imperfect because it was an earthly copy of a heavenly reality. The proof is that the sacrifices had to be performed again and again—showing that these offerings were unable definitively to atone for sin (9:25–26; 10:11). With Christ the foreshadowing and copying has ended. He acts not in the earthly copy but in the heavenly reality. "For Christ [the high priest] has entered, not into a sanctuary made with hands, a copy of the true one, but into heaven itself, now to appear in the presence of God on our behalf" (9:24).

The reading of today states that Christ as high priest of the new order has entered through the outer tent into the inner tent, the Holy of Holies, with his own blood and not with the blood of animals. Unlike the endlessly repeated—hence inadequate—sacrifices of old, it is done once for all (*ephapax*), because he remains everlastingly at the throne of God (vv. 11–12). The a fortiori argument, from the lesser to the greater instance ("How much more"), is intended to give Christians assurance that their consciences are cleansed. They are thus able to serve the living God (vv. 13–14). V. 15 is dense. In the old covenant, that of Sinai mediated by Moses, Israel was called to receive an inheritance, the land of Canaan. Israel's sin prevented them from a permanent ("eternal") possession of the land. But in the new covenant mediated by Jesus transgressions are once and for all removed by the death of Jesus. Therefore the people can look forward to eternal possession of their inheritance, "rest," possession of heaven.

Hebrews, then, declares that the ancient institutions are surpassed. They were only copies and shadows of a reality that now has appeared in perfection. Christ displaying his own blood in atonement dwells eternally before God. "When he had made

*For views of the tabernacle and ark which differ widely from Dr. Clifford's, see Gerhard von Rad, *Old Testament Theology,* trans. D. M. G. Stalker (New York: Harper & Row, Publishers), vol. 1, *The Theology of Israel's Historical Traditions* (1962), pp. 234ff.; and Brevard S. Childs, *The Book of Exodus,* Old Testament Library (Philadelphia: Westminster Press, 1974), pp. 529ff.—Ed.

purification for sin, he sat down at the right hand of the Majesty on high'' (1:3). The new covenant is firm.

Gospel: John 12:1–11. The synoptic gospel tradition records two distinct scenes of a woman anointing Jesus. The scene in Mark 14:3–9 (upon which Matt. 26:6–13 wholly depends) tells of an unnamed woman at the house of Simon the Leper at Bethany who anoints the head of Jesus with precious perfume. Jesus defends the woman's action against the indignation of some people. Luke (7:36–38) sets the anointing scene in Galilee where a sinful woman weeps at the feet of Jesus. After wiping his feet with her hair, she anoints them. The scandalous action of loosing the hair in public accounts for the Pharisee's indignation. Already in Luke's account there seems to be a mixing of some details from the Marcan tradition—the name of Simon and the introduction of perfume. John's account (12:1–8) apparently reflects a crisscrossing in oral transmission of the two stories. Essentially John's story is that of Bethany, to which have been incorporated details of the Lucan form, notably the anointing of the feet. Anointing of the feet with perfume is without parallel. One anointed the head, not the feet. But the detail suits John's purpose and is left in.

Unlike Mark and Matthew who place the scene after Jesus' entry into Jerusalem, John places it before the entrance, and with vv. 9–11 it forms the transition to the acclamation of the crowds in 12:12–19. The supper scene is set with the characters from the immediately preceding raising of Lazarus from the dead—Martha, Mary, and Lazarus (vv. 1–3). Jesus' raising of his friend to life in chap. 11 stirred belief in him but also set in motion forces seeking his death (11:45–53, 57). The crisis of belief and unbelief is present in this scene as Jesus sits amid believing friends and a disbelieving enemy—Judas. Mary anoints Jesus' feet with precious aromatic perfume (v. 3). He interprets it as anointing for his burial. The elliptical phrase in v. 7, ''Let her alone, let her keep it for the day of my burial,'' seems to mean that (unwittingly) she had been keeping it until now to embalm Jesus.

The gesture, related to Christ's life-giving to Lazarus and to his death, provokes hostile criticism from Judas who complains that the perfume might have been sold and the money given to the poor.

It is only a pretext and shows the lying nature of those who oppose Jesus. Even in the midst of friends to whom he has given life in a miraculous way, the murderous opposition of those who refuse his life-giving touch shows itself in Judas.

Vv. 9–11 are the immediate transition to the triumphal entry into Jerusalem. The verses take the story outside the friendly household into the public arena. The attitudes triggered by Lazarus' raising again surface. Some of the crowd came to see Lazarus and perhaps to come to belief in Jesus (v. 9), while others find the incident an incentive to put Jesus to death (vv. 10–11, and cf. 11:53).

The life-giving Jesus then is touched by the shadow of death on the eve of his public life. He provokes people to belief or to unbelief in the public forum and even in the circle of the disciples. As vulnerable and as victimized as he now appears, this faithful servant will reveal the justice of God which is saving to all the world.

HOMILETICAL INTERPRETATION

The week is under way, the working round begun. Now the Holy Week task of the preacher and the congregation are cast in somewhat different terms. The long Palm Sunday morning allowed time for the full range of worship: music and meditation, corporate prayer, the proclamation and hearing of the Word, the giving and receiving of the holy meal. Now all of that must be squeezed into a smaller space: A Eucharist at an ascetically early hour in the day? A noonday service before a hurried lunch? Something in the evening after a wearying, possibly dispiriting day? Whatever happens, whenever it happens, the keeping of Holy Week on this Monday will be very different from what happened on the day before.

First Lesson: Isa. 42:1–9. The beginning of Monday's worship, scripturally, is one of the splendidly numinous poems from Second Isaiah known as the servant songs. Who *is* this exemplar of whom the poems speak? Who is this one in whom immeasurable patience and triumphant righteousness are met? What has he to do with us in our workaday lives?

It turns out that there are no easy answers. The identity of the servant has been a topic of debate among scholars of the prophetic literature for most of this century. (See exegesis.) The texts themselves require inference. At no point is the servant given clear name or title (other than "servant"), and nothing in the literature speaks precisely enough about his actions to allow for a firm conclusion.

The issue is further clouded by the gospel's identification of *Jesus* with the servant songs. About that identification there is another kind of debate, although there is a clear concurrence that the servant songs meant very much to the writers of the NT and their depiction of Jesus.

In a way, the inconclusive debates leave the servant in anonymity, a nameless piece of the prophet's song to Israel about the promises and expectations of God.

So it is that God's word often comes, through the anonymous figures whose words and lives expose the real purposes of the Holy One.

"My servant," the Lord says, ". . . he will not call out or lift his voice high or make himself heard in the open street" (Isa. 42:1–2). It seems such a contrary thing. We are grown accustomed in our curious race to believing that the only things that really count in our lives together are the things that are publicly recognized: visible things, words and actions that are broadcast on the evening news. When of course the real truth, about who we are, about who we are meant to be, commonly resides in quiet, brave anonymity. The word from Isaiah about the servant of the Lord, the word that is spoken into the hurly-burly of our Holy Week, is that his promise and purpose more often than not come into creation in a hushed voice.

That quiet news is something to hear in whatever congregation is gathered in this bluest of Mondays. That we—even *we*—might be the unknown servants of God's intent should be heard as a counsel both of comfort and of challenge. It is a comfort because by it we are made the certified carriers of the only message that counts for anything at all. It is challenge because by it we are given to know that the blind—even those with excellent vision—are not forever condemned to blindness. It is the word that cuts through every chain of bondage, every neurosis, every instance of political captivity, every binding punishment of this world's life. The power for all of that freedom is invested not in the obvious authorities but in the servants who hear the servant, the anonymous ones who are blessed to have been given the word that sets people free.

Second Lesson: Heb. 9:11–15. The encounter of God and his creation, of the divine heart of the universe with the broken and imperfect human heart, can be only partly understood on the human side. "Now we see only puzzling reflections in a mirror," says Paul. And again, "[Now] my knowledge is partial" (1 Cor. 13:12). Because that is so, people of faith are left with the poor tools of human imagination: the analogies and metaphors that arise out of the best and truest of their experiences of God. Thus, as Auden once observed, "Theologians are in the difficult position of having to use language, which by its nature is anthropomorphic, to deny anthropomorphic conceptions of God" (W. H. Auden, *A Certain World* [New York: Viking Press, William Cole Books, 1970]).

Yet we have only language—borne up by music and by all of art—so we must make it succeed by putting it in the service of those encounters with God that mean most in our lives. So it was that the writer of the Letter to the Hebrews turned to the experience of worship, to the Hebrews' sacred Day of Atonement liturgy, and in it he sought an analogy that might somehow suggest the experience of God in Christ. Just preceding this Second Lesson the writer rehearses the action of the liturgy, reminding the reader of its content and its purposes. Then he seems to say, "All of that emblematic activity, all that sacred coming and going in the temple, is now surpassed and fulfilled by the saving, transforming action of God's own priest, Christ himself." At the heart of the liturgy was sacrifice. For the author of the Letter to the Hebrews, in this passage, Christ is the sacrifice of God.

The sacrifice of God. It is an immense suggestion, a colossal notion, and one that is completely at odds with what every sensible religion has always claimed: Human beings sacrifice for the sake of gods, *not* the other way round!

But the experience of Christians is what it is. In that experience is the clear sense that by the bloody events of a holy week God has once and for all sided with us, joined his life to our lives, taken on himself even the murderous impulses that are our shame.

The sacrifice of God. Of course the words refer to one death at one time in the history of the planet, of the cosmos. Can that distant death bear meaning in this week, in this year? Only in this: that the sacrificial willingness of God to die proclaims forevermore that the way to freedom from death is the way of sacrifice. It is the way of the one who went up to Jerusalem to death on a cross.

Gospel: John 12:1–11. A commonplace of our language is the reference to emergency circumstances, where human existence is imperiled, as "life-or-death" circumstances. "It's a matter," we say, "of life or death." It is not a phrase that is applied to much that happens in the commonplace comings and goings of our days, and yet there is a sense in which every day is full of life-or-death matters, life-or-death choices, life-or-death actions. "This day," says Moses to the gathered assembly of Israel, "I offer you the choice of life or death, blessing or curse" (Deut. 30:19). What that means is that what you do, with the things and the time and the self that you have, brings you down on the side of life, or else it brings you down on the other side, the side of death.

Jesus of Nazareth stood very much in the tradition of Moses and his teaching about life and death. Over and over again by what he said and what he did, he endorsed life: by his impatience with scribal allegiance to a dead letter of law when people were hungry and in need; by his ministry of healing, through which diseased bodies were made whole and social outcasts were restored to a natural companionship with their fellow creatures; by the restoration to life of one Lazarus. Sometime after that last act in behalf of life, Jesus is described in John's Gospel as having gone to be with Lazarus at a party. Of all things, Jesus of Nazareth stopping on his way to the Golgotha cross in order to go to a party! It is a splendid, life-filled image. There he sat, next to a gratefully living-and-breathing Lazarus, taking in the festivities. In the midst of things one of the women doing the serving bent over the feet of the honored guest and bathed and rubbed them with an extravagant perfumed oil. There is no record of Jesus' first reaction to this remarkable act, but the testy Judas is quoted in outrage. He saw the whole business as a waste, as a needless and pointless act. (Or perhaps, as John interprets, he wanted the valuable oil for his own purposes.) In any case the act is challenged. Jesus saw it as a choice for life, a work of extravagant hospitality offered while yet there was time. There is of course the prophetic nuance, by which the woman points ahead to the anointed body of the crucified one (see exegesis), but there is another kind of prophecy as well. It is the strong prophetic word that calls us to act in our days so that we choose life, celebrating it openly and extravagantly in the presence of the One from whom every mercy, and all life, comes.

Tuesday in Holy Week

Lutheran	Roman Catholic	Episcopal	Pres/UCC/Chr	Meth/COCU
Isa. 49:1-6	Isa. 49:1-6	Isa. 49:1-6	Isa. 42:1-9	Isa. 49:1-9a
Cor. 1:18-25		1 Cor. 1:18-31	1 Tim. 6:11-16	1 Cor. 1:18-31
John 12:20-36	John 13:21-33, 36-38	John 12:37-38, 42-50 or Mark 11:15-19	John 12:37-50	John 12:37-50

EXEGESIS

All three readings speak of the salvation offered to the chosen people that is also made available to the "nations," that is, non-Jews. They stress in their different ways that the offer to the nations is not due to their virtue but to the mysterious and widening circle of God's love, occasioned by the Jewish failure to recognize the new approach of God through his servant.

First Lesson: Isa. 49:1-6. The first reading is the second of the servant songs (on which see under Monday). Careful attention must be paid to the form or genre of the passage. It is a call narrative like those of Moses (Exod. 3:1—4:17), Gideon (Judges 6), and particularly Jeremiah (Jer. 1:4-10). In this type of narrative, the call to lead the people in crisis comes to a person who is reluctant to accept the commission. The person's reluctance can come from a speech defect (Moses), the ineloquence of youth (Jeremiah), lack of social position (Gideon), or in this passage, from a record of discouraging failure. "But I said, 'I have labored in vain, I have spent my strength for nothing and vanity'" (v. 4). In the type, the called one's resistance has to be overcome by appropriate divine words and deeds of assurance. Gideon is shown the dry and wet fleece (Judg. 6:36–40); Moses is given Aaron as his spokesman (Exod. 4:10–17); Jeremiah is furnished with divine words (Jer. 1:1–10). In our passage the discouragement of the servant, expressed in v. 4, must be overcome just as in the narratives of Moses, Gideon, and Jeremiah. The precise reassurance comes as a widening of the servant's responsibility to include the nations (v. 6).

Examining the dramatic structure of the passage, one finds first of all that the nations are summoned to hear the servant's commission (v. 1). Elsewhere in Second Isaiah, the nations are summoned to learn that their gods are powerless and that Israel is the people of the one true God, and so here. Israel's restoration invites them to acknowledge Israel's God as the only saving God. Vv. 1b–3 make use of old royal and prophetic language in which the prophet or king is publicly designated for mission. The vocabulary especially recalls Jer. 1:4–10. In the ancient Near East, politics was based on personal loyalties, and relationships between rulers were often stated in the language of loyalty and love. God's loving protection of his servant is beautifully expressed here. There are no textual or metrical reasons for excising the word "Israel" in v. 3. V. 4 records the prophet's past discouragement but also his trust (v. 4b). V. 5 resumes v. 1 as if to extend that original commission. The servant allows divine strength to be where he had felt weakness before (v. 5d, "my God has become my strength," relates one to v. 4, "I have spent my strength for nothing"). Climactically in v. 6 Yahweh declares the servant's role is not only to restore the survivors of the devastation of the Exile but also to become a light to the nations. The latter phrase should not be taken in too maximalist a sense. At this stage, Israel is not to preach to the nations so that they too may come and share in its privilege as God's people. Rather Israel's very existence as a restored people will show to the world that Israel's God is the only powerful God. The nations' own gods are thus shown to be no-gods, and the way is left open for them to acknowledge the saving power of Yahweh.

In this passage, then, the nations look on while the poor servant, true Israel, is given a commission by its loving and protecting God so that his salvation can reach to the ends of the earth.

Second Lesson: 1 Cor. 1:18–31. More so than in any other letter of Paul, 1 Corinthians shows the crises of a young and turbulent church shaping Paul's theology. Paul knew the port city very well since he had stayed there for a year and a half, ca. A.D. 51. During the spring of 57 he heard that various parties had sprung up, each based on allegiance to different founding figures—Cephas, Apollos, and even Paul. Such boasting of a human founder is abhorrent to Paul. It empties the cross of Christ of its power by making the foundation of belief the human qualities of the preacher. Paul focuses on the cross—the symbol of human powerlessness—to summarize his message. The cross is powerful not because of the wisdom of a human founder. Christianity is not just another philosophy beloved of the Greeks.

In vv. 18–25, Paul develops his arguments in superbly constructed antitheses. What is folly to man—the word of the cross—is the power of God. The proclamation of Christ crucified is not a new philosophical doctrine to be set alongside philosophies such as Stoicism or Epicureanism. These latter were systematic world views from which behavioral maxims were drawn. They often were taught by masters who exemplified their teaching. The word of the cross however is not primarily taught but preached. It is accepted as the word of God, not assented to because of its reasonableness. The word when preached is powerful with a power that comes from the word, and not from the virtue of the preacher. Paul appeals in v. 19 to a passage in the eighth-century prophet Isaiah. God there announces he will do a powerful new deed in the midst of a disbelieving people, which will make perish the wisdom of the wise (a particular class of teachers in Israel). When God acts, self-enclosed human activity falls uselessly away. In a series of rhetorical questions, Paul asks where mere human wisdom has been in the divine activity of the past and concludes it has been ineffectual (vv. 20–21). Then equating the Greek quest for philosophic salvation with the Jewish quest for signs of divine power—quests bound to fail—Paul proposes Christ crucified as the true sign of divine power and true saving wisdom (vv. 22–24). But only those Jews and Greeks who are *called* will find the word of the cross saving (v. 24). Thus does Paul preserve the divine initiative over against prideful human attempts at self-salvation.

In vv. 26–31, to prove his point that human strength alone cannot save, Paul daringly asks the Corinthians to consider their own lack of what the Greek world considered essential to the good life. By so illustrating his conviction that their salvation comes from God alone, Paul cleverly returns to the real beginning of his discourse in vv. 10–17. Because their very situation of earlier poverty proclaims God as their sole benefactor, they should not boast of Paul, Apollos, or Cephas, but only of Christ, who has become their wisdom and power. Paul thus memorably states that God has brought to nothing every human boast by showing his saving power in the very weakness and ignorance humans are wont to despise.

Gospel: John 12:37–50. The passage is the conclusion to 1:19—12:50, the first part of the Gospel. Vv. 37–43 draw upon primitive Christian reflections concerning the deeply troubling fact of the Jews' rejection of Jesus. For the most part, John adapts OT passages which speak of the Israelites' incomprehension or rejection of God. V. 37 rephrases Deut. 29:2–4, "You have seen all that the Lord did before your eyes in the land of Egypt . . . the signs, and those great wonders; but to this day the Lord has not given you a mind to understand, or eyes to see, or ears to hear." V. 38 speaks of the incredulity which the servant in Second Isaiah met. Vv. 40–41 refer to First Isaiah's inaugural vision of the glory of the Lord in Isaiah 6 which included in it a prediction that the prophet's preaching would meet with unbelief. In these expressions of the rejection of salvation by his own people—a rejection spoken in the prologue to the Gospel (1:11)—there is no denial of human freedom, either corporate or individual. Rather John and other early Christian thinkers such as Paul in Romans 9—11, shocked at the rejection of Jesus by his own people, looked to the authoritative Scriptures, the Old Testament, for an explanation. There they found the record of Israelite obstinacy. They concluded that Israel's failure to believe in Jesus was somehow included in the divine plan. It thus was no indication that Jesus was not the one sent by God. In vv. 42–43, John adds his own condemnation of those Jewish authorities who believed in Jesus but through fear of disapproval did not publicly confess him.

Vv. 44–50 are an unattached discourse of Jesus used now as a summary of the first part of the book. Its themes have appeared before, notably in 3:16–19. Vv. 44–45, in the poetic prose beloved of John, are in parallel. To believe is to see, and to believe in Jesus is to be in relationship to the Father who sends Jesus. One comes into the light, v. 46. Vv. 47–48 state the consequences of disbelief—judgment. Here is combined both realized and final eschatology. John usually stresses realized eschatology, that is, one is "judged," or situated definitively before God, by one's belief or disbelief in Jesus today. To believe is to become now a child of the light. To disbelieve is to remove oneself from community with the Father, Jesus, and the disciples. But final eschatology appears in v. 48. Jesus' word that invites today will condemn the disbeliever on the last day. Vv. 48–50 echo the Deuteronomic discourse of Moses in which the people are told that God will punish their failure to obey the messenger's word (Deut. 18:18–19; 31:19, 26). In Deut. 32:46–47, Moses tells the people that the authoritative words he speaks are their very life, by which they will live. To hearken to Jesus' words and to believe in him is to enter into relation to him and his Father and thus to live.

In these two summary passages in John, then, one finds somber reflection on a people's rejection of Jesus combined with an impressive statement of the possibility for all people to believe in Jesus and thus enter into communion with the Father.

HOMILETICAL INTERPRETATION

What is the church really meant to be about in a world so largely indifferent to its life and purposes? How is the church supposed to *be* the church, in Holy Week or any other week? In another century, in another culture, the answers may have been clear, but in our time and place there is great uncertainty. In our confusion we have confected a number of roles for the church to play in the social theater: Dispenser of Ceremonial, Demi-psychiatrist, Curator of the Great Tradition, Inflamer of Social Conscience. In each of these, and more, we have managed to keep faith with some true element in our calling, but we have also contributed greatly to the uncertainty about our vocation in a suffering world.

First Lesson: Isa. 49:1-6. The lessons for this Holy Week Tuesday speak to the question of the church's true purposes in an indifferent society. They begin with another of the songs of the servant from Second Isaiah—in which the servant is called and commissioned—and end with John's ringing description of Jesus' understanding of his mission: "What the father has said to me, therefore—that is what I speak" (John 12:50 NEB).

In the prophetic figure that is Second Isaiah there appear two powerful allegiances: to the Lord who speaks and to the people who are meant to hear. On the one hand the ministry of the prophet is simply to be God's voice, to proclaim God's word, willy-nilly. The whole of the prophetic tradition in the OT attests to a kind of irresistible compulsion in the prophet, such that he is literally unable to shut up. When Jeremiah tried to be silent, the Lord's word burned within him until he spoke it (Jer. 20:9). "The Lord God has spoken," said Amos; "who can but prophesy?" (Amos 3:8). So it is with the prophet whose message is of servanthood. He is not confident to proclaim, nor bold in believing, that he can be the instrument of the divine will. Indeed, he passes through a darkness of believing that all that he has done and said amounts to nothing save vanity and aimlessness (49:4). Yet somehow in his closeness to God he is reassured, given what he needs of patience and courage to speak the word he is given to speak.

There is in the image of the uncertain prophet some counsel for an uncertain church. It is the first work of the people of God to wait upon his word and then, in the reassurance of his presence, to speak it. Not that it will be noticed. "In the secular world in which I live," a young woman wrote at the beginning of one Lent not long ago, "it is perfectly possible for Lent to pass all but unnoticed: one day some people on the street have ashes on their foreheads, and awhile later it is suddenly Easter." So it is for the church in an indifferent society. Yet the task is what it is: to put wit and faith in the service of God's word, however irrelevant that word may seem to the ear of an insouciant world. That is the first charge to the church and to the preacher.

But there is another charge, no less demanding. It is the charge by which the prophet is bound to the people he addresses. Israel's prophets knew painful ambiguity because of their close relationship to the people to whom they spoke Yahweh's judging, saving word (see exegesis). Set apart for the particular work of a prophet, Second Isaiah was at the same time *of* the people.

So it must be for the church. The word that comes from without, that is entrusted to church and preacher, must nevertheless be spoken from within. However disinterested the hearers may seem, the word is still a word *for* them, a word to heal and comfort, a word to challenge and save. So that church and preacher do not become indifferent, the truth in that charge must never be lost. It is precisely in our recollection that we are meant *both* to proclaim *and* to sit among those to whom the proclamation is delivered that we discover our calling to be servants.

Second Lesson: 1 Cor. 1:18–31. The issues of the fundamental mission and purpose of the church—of who church members are meant to be and what they are meant to do—occur in this Second Lesson in the form of Paul's flat-footed advice to Corinthian Christians. Significantly, although his language is candid and strong, what he says is said as a knowing pastor. It is clear that the people to whom he writes, however disputatious among themselves, however misled, are people about whom he very much cares. ("I am always thanking God for you," he says, 1 Cor. 1:3.) It is evidently necessary to speak words of criticism and admonition, but they are words spoken by one who cares for the people who are the objects of his counsel. "Caring matters most," Baron von Hügel wrote in one of his remarkable letters to his niece. There is a sense in which that observation might well be hung over the preacher's desk. The proclamation of the gospel that was given to Paul to make, the proclamation that is given to every preacher, may be enhanced by wit and charm and a resonant voice, but in order truly to be the proclamation it must have its root in caring.

The Corinthians about whom Paul cared had apparently yielded to a temptation that has plagued the church from the beginning. They had taken the astonishing truth of the gospel and reduced it to an ideology. Of course it is a powerful temptation. In a world of attractive and competing ideologies it is not easy to resist getting into the fray with some version of the faith that might, at least, draw a crowd. "If we cannot construct for ourselves a *new* ideology out of the elements of the Christian story," church people have been given to say over twenty centuries, "let us at least put the faith in the service of some going ideal we can admire and support!" So, in turn, social theories and political systems and economic theses and principles of ethics and aesthetics—all products of the "wisdom of men"—have attracted the affectionate support of Christians, even to a willingness to equate a human system with the gospel.

But the gospel is not an ideology among ideologies, nor can any human system of thought contain its truths. The gospel we are given, by which the church is meant to define its mission and understand its purposes, is the quite *un*ideological claim that God loves us and that the sign of his love is a cross. That claim renders all ideological disputes beside the point. Moreover, it is a claim that is made upon the whole church, upon every member. To proclaim the sacrificing love of God is the work of the whole church, a work very often done more by the examples of simple people than by hierarchs and theologians. It is a work, this task of bespeaking God's love with lips and lives, about which it is thrilling to be reminded in the midst of this Holy Week.

Gospel: John 12:37–50. At the heart of the Holy Week story is rejection. It is the cruel compound of misunderstanding with envy and fear and indifference. It occurs, in one way or another, in every life. Even in the most intimate and trust-dependent of our relationships there lurks the threat of rejection, the possibility that our opinions and ideas—perhaps our very selves—will be spurned and excluded.

In John's summary of the public ministry of Jesus of Nazareth which is today's Gospel lesson the theme is rejection. The author seeks some cause, some explanation for the repudiation which led to the cross. He includes also a reflection on judgment, on the ultimate outcome for the repudiators. Taken together, they are two sides of one theme and they ring of the conviction that judgment resides in the Lord of history, the God of the prophets whose word of saving judgment is the last word.

That conviction must have been the conviction of Jesus. Holding to it, he faced into the storm of ridicule and contempt. There may have been surprise at first, that the very people who ought first to have received him with a shout of welcoming joy turned on him instead with snarls of refusal. If there was surprise it passed quickly. For Jesus knew the history of the rejection of the word of God. He knew the sorry tale of Amos's banishment and the painful account of the harassment of Jeremiah; he remembered the resignation to rejection and suffering by Isaiah's foreshadowing servant. The rejection of Jesus is a kind of seal upon the truth that he is in the line of Israel's prophets, charged to speak God's word—to *be* God's word—in the face of obstinate refusal.

There is an editorial aside following on this perception of the inevitability of the rejection of Jesus. In it the Gospel writer observes that in fact quite a few people, including some who were "in authority" (12:42) did believe in him, *did* somehow sense in him the truth about who God is, about who they were meant to be. But fear kept them from saying so; fear of being tarred themselves with the brush of scorn; fear that the sacrifice of the security of this world's glory was not worth the risk of heavenly glory. John names no names, and the commentators suggest that his editorializing has a dubious historical basis. But it is an insertion capable of touching us just the same. We know about keeping quiet, even when we sense that the truth may not be spoken unless we speak it. We know about the fear of scorn, about the passion for acceptance by our fellow creatures, no matter what the cost. So we may be touched by the reference to the anonymous ones who, though believing, dared not speak. Let them remind us, in this Holy Week, of what shame it may be to keep the silence of denial in the presence of the Word.

It seems generally agreed that the concluding verses of this section (12:44–50) represent a kind of précis of the primary elements in the life and ministry of Jesus, the life and ministry that were rejected. In the little compass of six verses Jesus is set forth as the one by whom God is known: not known *about* or partly known, but fully and truly known. He is the unmistakable light which illumines the life which is at the heart of the universe. All that he taught and said and did, all that he is as he wanders among that bewildered and contemptuous lot of his fellow human beings, all of it was meant to irradiate the life of God.

That is still the mission of Christ, done now through his body the church. It is our mission: to expend all of our words and all of our deeds so that we may shed light, not on our poor lives, but on the saving life of God.

Wednesday in Holy Week

Lutheran	Roman Catholic	Episcopal	Pres/UCC/Chr	Meth/COCU
Isa. 50:4–9a	Isa. 50:4–9	Isa. 50:4–9a	Isa. 52:13—53:12	Isa. 50:4–9
Rom. 5:6–11		Heb. 9:11–15, 24–28	Rom. 5:6–11	Rom. 5:6–11
Matt. 26:14–25	Matt. 26:14–25	John 13:21–35 or Matt. 26:1–5, 14–25	Luke 22:1–16	John 13:21–38 or Matt. 26:1–5, 14–25

EXEGESIS

The readings today are united in their attention to the death of the servant and its redemptive power. The Isaian and Matthean excerpts speak of the betrayal of the innocent just person into the hands of sinners. That the betrayal is not unto death but means life for the people is very explicitly affirmed by Paul.

First Lesson: Isa. 50:4–9. In the third of the four servant songs (see under Monday), the servant is portrayed as a faithful disciple and teacher (vv. 4–6) who is confident of divine support and vindication in persecution (vv. 7–9). The prophet expresses his inner drama of openness to God's word, his experience of physical abuse and humiliation from his uncomprehending fellows, and his ultimate trust in vindication. This revelation of personal struggle is not mere autobiography. Rather it is rooted in the individual psalm of lament, the most frequent type in the Psalter. In these psalms the psalmist typically calls out to God, displaying in generalized terms of distress his desperate plight so that God who cares for the poor and distressed will rescue him. An intrinsic part of the psalm is a statement of trust in his just and caring God. Jeremiah, some seventy years before Second Isaiah, adapted the individual psalm of lament for his prophetic ministry. By making public his own inner anguish before God, Jeremiah gave his people a paradigm of behavior in the crisis that they must soon undergo in the destruction of the temple and in the Exile.

In Second Isaiah's use of the individual lament, the prophet records the anguish of a loyal servant and in so doing provides for Israel a model for the behavior of true servants. The word *servant* in Israel meant one close to and sharing responsibility with God or the king or highly placed person. The servant says in vv. 4–5 that he is loyal, hearing—that is, obeying—all that the master teaches.

His loyalty as a servant-disciple costs him the esteem of his fellows, and punishment (v. 6). In the second part of the poem (vv. 7–9), the servant's trust in his Lord makes him able to bear the shame (v. 7, read "but" for RSV "for"). In the psalms of lament the troubles of the psalmist were often legal ones, especially unjust accusation in court. The servant makes use of the traditional lawcourt vocabulary. He declares the judge is on his side (vv. 8–9a). "The one who vindicates me" literally is "the one who declares me innocent," that is, the judge. His enemies cannot stand up in court.

By generously making available his own inner experience of hopeful fidelity to the Lord amid the disbelief and ridicule of his peers, the prophet becomes himself a living example of servanthood to all Israel. Armed only with his faith in the loving and just God who protects his servants, the servant can stand up boldly against all that is sinful and violent.

Second Lesson: Rom. 5:6–11. Though the position of the unit 5:1–11 within Romans is disputed, some holding that it concludes the first part (1:16—4:25), it is perhaps best to see this section as an introduction to the second part, chaps. 5—11. These verses state the main theme that is later developed: the love of God which transforms the justified person through Jesus Christ. In 1:16—4:25, Paul showed how the righteousness of God justifies the believer through the gospel. Now Paul explores the dimensions of the reconciled life, which is called "peace with God through our Lord Jesus Christ" (5:1). From this conviction of being in the sphere of grace, that is, in the salvific regard of God, the Christian makes a threefold boast: in his or her confidence in a glorious future (v. 2), in present sufferings since they are not ultimately destructive to the relationship with Christ (vv. 3–5), and in God through Christ, the Christian's reconciliation (v. 11). The threefold boast unifies the passage.

In vv. 6–11, Paul assures the Christian that justification is not a single action, an existence without possibilities of further movement. It has rather established a firm basis for a richer relationship. To show the richness of life in Christ after initial justification, the apostle uses an a fortiori argument. If something is true in a weak case, how much more true is it in a stronger case. If God showed his love so powerfully when we were sinners, how much more now that we are justified. The wrath of God from which we are saved in v. 9 is a specialized biblical term. It does not refer to the anger of a capricious deity but to the all-holy God's withdrawal from a culpably sinful situation. God's absence was often for a specified time. At the appropriate time God would turn once again to his people, moved by his own love and fidelity. God ends his absence from his people by sending his Son, through whom he draws close in reconciliation. The verses show therefore that the death of Christ remains the sign of God's love and the source of God's love for the justified Christian.

Gospel: Matt. 26:14–25. At a very early stage in the formation of the gospel tradition the passion account had come to be fixed. So central was the death of Jesus in early Christian preaching that it was imperative the story be set down early and authoritatively. One concern of the very early pre-Marcan narrative was to show that the death of the Messiah at the hands of sinners had been ordained by God and also accepted by Jesus, who was portrayed as the ideal suffering just person. Otherwise his premature death might look like divine judgment against him and his preaching. He would be ranked alongside those numerous messiahs who appeared in Palestine around that time only to perish in violent uprisings.

In Matthew's Gospel, written probably in the 70s of the first century, one finds more or less the same fixed passion account as in the other Gospels. Vv. 14–25 tell the story of Judas in a fashion similar to Mark. In vv. 14–16 Judas, expressly called "one of the Twelve," arranges with the chief priests to hand over Jesus. Matthew dramatizes the scene by dialogue. The price of betrayal is thirty pieces of silver, apparently the price of a slave in the OT (Zech.

11:12 and Exod. 21:32). With disaster looming the passion meal is prepared (vv. 17–19). Jesus is clearly aware of his fate, as is evident from Matthew's "My time is at hand. At your house do I celebrate" (v. 18).

In vv. 20–25, the third scene in the Judas drama, betrayal of the just person by his friend is underlined. That the betrayal took place during solemn table sharing would be extremely important in the East. It is a painful situation powerfully expressed in the lament psalm: "Even my bosom friend, the one whom I trusted, the one who ate at my table, has lifted up his heel against me" (Ps. 41:9). Jesus knows the treachery beforehand, as the gesture of both himself and Judas dipping hands in the bowl at the same time shows. V. 24 says explicitly that the Son of man's death is according to the Scriptures, that is, the OT. No specific Scripture is cited, but the reader is probably referred to the psalms of the innocent just person in the Psalter. In those poems the psalmist is often the subject of unjust legal accusations (as Jesus will soon be) and of abandonment by friends. Like the loyal servant in Second Isaiah he remains faithful to the God who called him even when it means betrayal by friends and public misunderstanding and humiliation. His only hope is God, who will vindicate him by resurrection.

HOMILETICAL INTERPRETATION

We are at the midpoint. After today the drama intensifies, deepening and darkening like a starless night. There is a sense in which the lessons for this day prepare us for that darkness, alerting us to the truth that even when there seems to be no light there can be meaning.

First Lesson: Isa. 50:4–9. The lessons begin with another song of the servant who suffers. Its meaning is simply that the suffering is not pointless. The servant recognizes that part at least of the vocation of serving is to suffer, and that the vocation and the suffering it contains are given purpose by God's participation in both. There is in the servant an inner strength that is born not of some self-generated stoicism but of an awareness that the Lord God "stands by to help me" (50:7).

Although it is not clear who this servant is, it is apparent that his servanthood is meant as a kind of paradigm. Seen in that way this passage, and each of the servant passages upon which Second Isaiah hangs his prophecy, become a word to us—first to Israel and then to the church—about the nature of our calling.

When these songs were first sung, of course, they were heard by a people in exile, threatened by rootlessness and confusion about what they were to believe and to do with their lives. To a people in such a condition the prophet gives the sample of the servant. Now that sample is set before us, a people also threatened by rootlessness and confusion about what to believe, about what to do with our lives.

Is it so remote from us, this high prototype of faithfulness? Can we not see here some clue about the life to which God calls us? In the image of the servant we, who breathe an atmosphere that reeks of the ambition to self-fulfillment and self-realization, are given a vision of faithfulness that is rooted in the willingness to serve not self but God. From that willingness there flows whatever is needed to find meaning in the darkness, courage in the struggle, patience for the outcome that is in the hand of a just God.

"Isn't it just too wonderful," writes a black South African priest, "in the midst of our anguishes, our impotence imagined and real, our tears and laughter, our poverty and affluence, our squalor and our luxury, our imprisonments—and our liberty—in the light and in the darkness God is with us."

Second Lesson: Rom. 5:6–11. The preparation to receive the gospel's news on Maundy Thursday and Good Friday includes remembering the source of our hope. In the sober gloom of Holy Week we need squarely to face the reality of rejection, even the rejection of Christ; but we need also to hold on to hope. We need to "reckon seriously," as John Macquarrie has put it, "with God's promise, as his utter commitment to his creation, so that he could never acquiesce in its total ruin; [and] with his power to resurrect, that is to say, to bring forth the new when all avenues seem closed" (*Christian Hope* [New York: Seabury Press, 1978], p. 111). It is in that reckoning that we may be made to discover that the dead ends of our days are not really dead at all. And that is so because even the cruelty that shapes the Holy Week story does not issue in a dead end. It issues instead in our justification.

We have been "justified by Christ's sacrificial death," says Paul. Justified. There is in the English word perhaps too much of the spirit of narrow, legalistic disputes. Of course Paul's Greek word came out of the lawcourts, having to do with determining who is the upright and law-abiding citizen and, by implication, who is not. Given that meaning, how can "justification" be the link between ourselves and the death of Christ? Paul goes to considerable lengths to answer that question, clinging throughout to the analogy from the law. It is not necessarily the preacher's Holy Week task to unravel Pauline theology on the matter. Perhaps it is enough to find in Paul's claim the basis for the hope of Holy Week. Paul's claim of justification, whatever else it may mean, speaks in the first place of our freedom. By God's extravagant mercy, held up before us in the events that lead to the cross, we are set free. Free, that is, from having to concoct our own definitions of righteousness, free from having to build systems that satisfy those definitions. By Christ's death we are let out of the prisons of every kind of self-definition and given a new standing, as upright and righteous and justified children of the King who is our judge. In that freedom is our everlasting hope.

Gospel: Matt. 26:14-25. The Gospel's word on this day is the narrative of betrayal. The crucial figure, the betrayer, acted under the cloak of friendship out of what were seemingly venal motives. Almost nothing else is known of him. He is said in one account to have come from a town, Kerioth, that is so obscure it is not mentioned anywhere else in literature. He is called Iscariot, a name—or a title—apparently without meaning. Even his death is obscure; the account of it in Acts 1 is open to a variety of interpretations. (Was it a suicide or some sudden illness? Was it a curse?) Here in the mid-point of the drama, this shadow of a man becomes the linchpin by which the ominous events are held together.

It would be an easy matter to fix all attention, all meditation, on Judas. But there is a hazard in that, and it is the hazard of locating sin too narrowly, of finding guilt in just one place. To do that is not only to overlook the network of human interaction which issues in evil acts, it is also to suggest that since evil can be certainly discoverable in one spot it must not be elsewhere. The truth of course is that what Auden once called the "dark counter-center" of human nature is a pervasive reality, occurring in each of us. If we were not actually acting toward a friend so as to insure his death, we surely are capable of some strange stirrings of delight when someone, even someone very close to us, is in distress. So far from being the single locus of evil is Judas Iscariot that it might even be said of him that his betrayal provides an illuminating sample of *all* betrayal. In his self-seeking, God-fleeing act we can see the shadows of our entire race in flight from the goodness of God.

There is another illumination in this narrative of Matthew's. It is the unambiguous light by which we are given to see God's confrontation with evil. Jesus acknowledges his betrayer and he pronounces his doom. In his words can be heard a pronouncement not just upon Judas (for whom it would have been better "if he had never been born," v. 25). It is also a judgment upon every betrayal of the Son of man, every assault upon the life of God as that precious life is found among us. This story, and the whole of the NT, says clearly that God's life is touched and affected by evil. It says also that in Christ can be found the supreme condemnation of evil and the ultimate triumph over it.

Maundy Thursday

Lutheran	Roman Catholic	Episcopal	Pres/UCC/Chr	Meth/COCU
Jer. 31:31–34	Exod. 12:1–8, 11–14	Exod. 12:1–14a	Num. 9:1–3, 11–12	Jer. 31:31–34 or Num. 9:1–3, 11–12
Heb. 10:15–39	1 Cor. 11:23–26	1 Cor. 11:23–26 (27–32)	1 Cor. 5:6–8	Heb. 10:16–39
Luke 22:7–20	John 13:1–15	John 13:1–15 or Luke 22:14–30	Mark 14:12–26	Luke 22:7–30 or John 13:1–17, 34

EXEGESIS

All three lessons contain expressions of the new covenant spoken of by Jeremiah. God will establish with Israel a new relationship which he will nurture with a surer presence than the first. The NT readings see the newness of the covenant in its ratification by Christ's blood (Hebrews) and in its power to draw the scattered people together into one people (Luke).

First Lesson: Jer. 31:31–34. Even after the northern kingdom of Israel had separated from the southern kingdom of Judah in 922 B.C., as a result of powerful and deeply rooted disintegrating forces, the prophets of Israel kept alive the hope of an eventual reunion of the tribes into one people of Yahweh. God has woven together diverse groups and traditions that they may be his people and he may be their God, according to the ancient phrase rooted in the Mosaic covenant traditions. For two hundred years—until Assyria's destruction of Samaria, the capital city of the northern kingdom, in 722—the prophets spoke to "all Israel" on the basis of the venerable common traditions. With King Josiah, who reigned over Judah from 640–609, there was a revival of the old national feeling. When Assyria declined, Josiah began to annex the northern territories into one kingdom, like that ruled by David centuries before.

The "book of consolation" (chaps. 30–33) records utterances of Jeremiah to the separated northern tribes during Josiah's opening to the north. Though there were doubtless southerners who harbored grudges from two centuries of hostility, Jeremiah is generous and full of hope in God's merciful power to unify. He assures the northern tribes that God has heard their cries. There will be a new covenant not dependent as the old was on the fragile link of parent teaching child. The Lord will initiate his people's knowledge of him. Jeremiah could easily have lent his prestige to Josiah's expansion and simply called upon the north to submit to the southern king. Instead he asks them to see in the turn of events the Lord meeting his people for a new covenant. They are to "turn," or to convert, as human beings must when God enters their lives in a new way.

In v. 31, "and the house of Judah" appears to be an addition to the original addressed only to the house of Israel. When Judah too suffered exile in the sixth century, the prophetic word was reformulated so as to address the whole people. The old covenant by which the people were united in allegiance to Yahweh no longer was valid because of Israel's disobedience to her husband, Yahweh

(v. 32). Jeremiah uses marital language familiar from the eighth-century northern prophet Hosea (Hos. 2:1–13). In v. 33, Jeremiah uses the old covenant formula, "I will be their God and they shall be my people," but in a new context appropriate to the radical newness of the relationship. The old need of parent teaching child of the covenant stipulations (Deut. 6:6–9, 20–25) will be replaced by the Lord inscribing all in the heart. To know the Lord in v. 34 means to be faithful to him. To be the Lord's people is by that fact to have their sins forgiven (v. 34).

The passage constitutes an authoritative announcement that the Lord takes the initiative in bringing back his people, dispersed by their own fault, into a unity. There is recognition that the human sinfulness that caused the rupture between God and people, and division among the tribes, will be healed by God's presence.

Second Lesson: Heb. 10:15–39. This long excerpt combines the end of the doctrinal exposé of the once-and-for-all nature of Christ's bloody sacrifice (8:1—10:18), an exhortation based in that doctrine to approach God in faith and love (10:19–31), and another exhortation (10:32–39), a preamble to the catalog of faith's heroes and heroines of chap. 11. This unusual juxtaposition of incomplete sections probably comes from the lectionary committee's desire to quote Jer. 31:33–34, the first reading—which is also echoed in the Lucan passage—as the introduction.

In the first section (see under Monday) the author uses an elaborate comparison of Christ's sacrifice with the propitiating ritual of the desert tabernacle. The desert tabernacle was thought to be a copy of the heavenly reality, deriving its efficacy from that heavenly exemplar. But Christ is now in the heavenly tabernacle where his powerful bloody sacrifice, once made, need never be repeated. Forgiveness of sin however is not the only effect of OT sacrifices nor of Christ's. Blood sacrifice also inaugurated the old covenant which failed. Christ's sacrifice initiates the new covenant which shall stand forever. The quote from Jeremiah describing the new covenant began the long doctrinal treatise (8:8–12). It also ends it, leaving in the reader's mind the enduring forgiveness of sin that is part of a permanent relation to God.

Vv. 19–31 are an exhortation. Using liturgical language, the author urges the Christian now purified to enter the sanctuary, confident in his or her access to God because of Christ the high priest. The purification enables the Christian to draw near to other members of the community as well (vv. 24–25). The seriousness of vv. 26–31 is based on the fact that there is now only one valid path to God—the way of Christ. Reject that—and there is no more hope.

Vv. 32–39 are another exhortation prefacing, it seems, the list of faith heroes in chap. 11. The past sufferings of the community in the days before they retreated from their original commitment are recalled. In view of a future in which they had confidence, they were faithful. Their faith is interpreted as fidelity, like the fidelity of Moses and of the faithful son in Heb. 3:5–6, and that in the particular Greek version of Hab. 2:3–4 quoted in vv. 37–38. So does the author wish to link his readers in their past faith to the great biblical heroes of the past in the section immediately following.

The reading as a whole urges Christians to act as befits an eternally covenanted people. The covenant is held out forever, too firmly rooted in God's fidelity to be negated by human sinfulness.

Gospel: Luke 22:7–20. We have already mentioned in discussing Matt. 26:14–25 that the passion framework has been schematized for easily understandable reasons even before the first of our gospels was written. Each evangelist could however organize the passion traditions with some freedom as is apparent in Luke's account of the supper. Vv. 7–13, to be sure, do not diverge much from Mark and Matthew except for minor rearrangements of Jesus' instructions and the specification of Peter and John as the two disciples referred to in Mark 14:13. Jesus' precise instructions to his disciples show his mastery over the details of the meal and underscore that it is he who presides over the Passover.

To understand the further nuances of the Lucan account, one must recall that Luke presents the kingdom of God as successively realized in defined stages. Though the kingdom "is in the midst of you" (17:21), that is, already at work among the disciples, it has a history that extends backward and forward. The first stage is the time of the Law and the Prophets culminating in the announcements to God-fearing Jews (Zechariah, Mary, the shepherds, Simeon) and in the preaching of John the Baptist (chaps. 1—3). The second stage is that of the Spirit-filled presence of Jesus (cf. especially 4:14–21) when the kingdom is preached and begins to take hold. The stage of the church comes next with the pivotal scenes of the ascension and of Pentecost. Jesus returns to heaven, and the apostles find themselves empowered to preach and do what Jesus preached and did (Acts of the Apostles). This latter will yield to the final age, the fullness of the kingdom of God. The periods are intimately related to each other, the early ones pointing to the later, and the later ones resuming and fulfilling the earlier.

The distinctiveness of the Lucan vis-à-vis the other synoptic accounts of the supper lies partly in the backward-forward perspective of vv. 15–22. This perspective becomes clear when the so-called longer text is adopted as is increasingly being done by modern scholars. The second edition of the RSV (1971) has adopted it. Though some manuscripts and hence some modern translations omit the latter part of v. 19 and all of v. 20, we assume them in this commentary. The verses are:

> 19 "(my body) which is given up for you. Do this as a remembrance of me." 20 And likewise the cup after they had eaten, saying, "This cup which is poured out for you is the new covenant in my blood."

What is the meaning of the longer text? We suggest tentatively that there is a deliberate contrast between the two cups, the cup of the old covenant in the Passover ritual (vv. 15–18) and the cup of the new covenant in the last supper (vv. 19–20). The Passover meal began with a blessing followed by a first cup of wine. The lamb was then eaten with herbs and haroseth, a bitter sauce. Following a second glass of wine, a designated "son" asked, "Why is this night different from all nights?" Then was recited the story of Israel's redemption in Egypt (chiefly contained in Exodus 1—15) and other stories detailing the formation of the people into the people of God. The first cup in vv. 17–18 seems to be the cup of this traditional meal. When Jesus says, "I tell you I shall not eat it until it is fulfilled in the kingdom of God," he is declaring that the Passover insofar as it is commemorative of past saving events only has come to an end. For him its value lies now in its functions of showing forth the future ingathering of Israel and of anticipating the final age. It was commonly believed that the Messiah would appear at

Passover and inaugurate the new age when the people would be liberated from their enemies and be invited to the messianic banquet.

In contrast to the first cup which has lost its traditional meaning, Luke describes the second cup. He uses phrases which come from the Pauline tradition (cf. 1 Cor. 11:23–26), "(my body) given up for you. Do this as a remembrance of me." The word "remembrance," used also of the Passover rite, makes it clear that Jesus intends his action to be a new rite for the time of the church. This rite of eating and drinking replaces the traditional Passover meal. Like the old it celebrates the past salvation of God but includes also the saving work of Jesus himself.

The Passover meal insofar as it celebrated the old saving deeds reaffirmed the bond uniting the people and their God. It made it possible for Jews to participate in the bonding between the people and their God described in the ceremony of Exodus 24. Moses and the seventy elders representing the people had ratified the Sinai covenant by eating and drinking. The blood had been ritually sprinkled on the people and on the altar (representing God), manifesting the uniting of people and Deity in sacred covenant. Luke describes the blood of Jesus as effecting a new covenant, alluding to the words of Jer. 31:31–34 ("new covenant") discussed under the First Lesson. The meal then is a covenant meal, and Jesus' death binds people and God into a new unity.

The new covenant meal is a ritual for the time of the church, when the disciples can participate in Jesus' powerful covenanting act and can anticipate the final ingathering of the people into the definitive unity of the final age. Resuming and fulfilling the old covenant, it dramatically illustrates how Jeremiah's new covenant is to be understood by Christians.

HOMILETICAL INTERPRETATION

This is the day of the meal. It is the day to recall with a special sensitivity the meaning of our gathering to take bread and wine in the refreshment we call Communion. The Gospel lesson from Luke describes the meal of which our meals are the reflection and remembrance. In that lesson, and in each of the lessons for Maundy

Thursday, God is spoken of as the one who shows himself and his purposes in new ways, surprising ways, ways without precedent.

First Lesson: Jer. 31:31–34. Much of the practice of religion of the ancient Near East was given over to attempts to manipulate the gods in order that they might behave predictably. The farmer and the herdsman prayed and sacrificed and believed so that the seasons might be regular and include the requisite amounts of rainfall and sunshine. Hebrew faith was of a different order. The people of the OT worshiped a God who could not be made to behave predictably, whose very being, indeed, proclaimed change and newness. They did not always remember this, of course, and the OT is filled with stories of people who attempted to control Yahweh, to reduce him to manageable proportions. Against those attempts the prophets raised their voices.

Jeremiah speaks the Lord's words: "I will make a new covenant with Israel . . . it will not be like the covenant I made with their forefathers" (31:31–32). At the moment when the politicians had cast the future according to their own best interests (see exegesis), Jeremiah speaks of the inbreaking of the peace of God. It is not a peace to satisfy partisan needs but a new peace, an inclusive peace, a peace that unpredictably settles equally upon victim and victor.

Such a peace is, surely, a part of the meaning of the eucharistic meal. The family of God gathers to be nourished for the work of establishing peace, the peace that insists upon justice and requires forgiveness. It is no easy work, but the God who speaks to us in the prophets, who comes to us in the meal, calls us to it and, by his new covenant, joins us in it.

Second Lesson: Heb. 10:15–39. Perhaps because the Letter to the Hebrews is itself a "learned sermon" (see Monday's exegesis) it can be an intimidation to the preacher. The author's theses are dense with ideas and he renders them in complex locutions, depending often on allusion and suggestion. To take a fragment of this difficult epistle and build upon it a modern sermon for a modern congregation can seem an immense undertaking. Still, it can be a task very much worth the travail. For the truth about the Letter to the Hebrews is that its labyrinth holds seminal theology, the fundamental truths of Christian faith. Today's Second Lesson is a sample of that.

Beginning in pedagogy (vv. 1–18) and ending in exhortation (vv. 19–39), the tenth chapter of Hebrews describes the cardinal realities of the Christian life: the work that God has accomplished in the priesthood of Jesus Christ, and the response that men and women are called upon to make in the light of that work. Everything else in the Christian life depends on our getting those two things straight. The *means* we use to get them straight may—perhaps must—change from generation to generation, and it is no small part of the preacher's task to lay hold upon the appropriate means for the time and place in which he or she is called to preach. The fundamental realities, however, remain the same: God's sacrificing love, offered once and for always in Christ Jesus, frees us from the old obligations of "doing" religion, so that we may instead be made alive by faith. The signs of that new freedom, that lively faith, are the signs of "love and active goodness" in a community marked by works of mutual encouragement.

It is apparent that the readers for whom this letter was originally meant had neglected those works in some significant ways. The preacher who writes to them takes on the task of recalling them to a discipline, reminding them that the God who frees them by his sacrificing love is also the one who judges them in their freedom. His language is strong, even threatening, but his purpose is less to intimidate his readers than to require of them the disciplines of selfless love and mutuality which are the emblems of the Christian life.

Is the role of disciplinarian one which the modern preacher should pursue? Most probably would avoid it. Yet the truth is that there *are* disciplines by which the community of professing Christ-followers are meant to live. When those disciplines are abandoned, *someone* needs to speak up and say so. On this day of sorrow and betrayal, the author of the Letter to the Hebrews speaks up to say that every act of self-interest and duplicity, every act that breaks the community instead of building it up, will be measured and judged by the God whose love requires love. The preacher is called to preach comfort to a comfortless world, but perhaps in that preaching there should be something of the spirit depicted in the last panel of the great Bayeux tapestry. The fine medieval cartoon portrays William the Conqueror on horseback, his lance gently sticking into the backside of the last man in a line of soldiers. The inscription reads, "William, comforting his troops."

Gospel: Luke 22:7–20. Here, at last, is the description of the meal. On this day of God's new possibilities and new commandments (*novum mandatum*—from whence Maundy) we are given Luke's version of the last meal that Jesus has with his friends. In Luke's telling of it the supper is clearly the Passover supper, the annual ritual by which every Jewish household celebrated God's participation in history in the freedom event of the Exodus. It is a supper both solemn and joyful and an occasion of extraordinary significance in Jewish life. The Jewishness of this last supper account is extremely clear. The preparation, the action at the table, even the words Jesus speaks, all are redolent with the Passover spirit. This is a meal taken in obedience to Jewish piety and practice. That it becomes the sponsor of something quite else in Christian piety and practice should not obscure its origins. Instead, let this account remind the Christian community of its origins in Judaism and of the continuing bond that Christians and Jews have in their worship of the God who acts to bring deliverance to the captives. The practice that has grown up in some places of Jews "teaching" Christians the custom of the Seder meal on Maundy Thursday can be a mere entertainment. At the same time, when it is seriously undertaken, it can profoundly enrich the keeping of this day in a Christian congregation.

There is a temptation to sentimentalize Maundy Thursday and the story that is at its heart. When that happens the cultic instincts take over and the action of the liturgy becomes a kind of pale recreation of the events around the table in that "large upper room." The preacher needs to speak a word against that temptation to sentimentality and to say something of the rich liveliness in the here and now which the meal provides. It *is* our central act of worship, and as such it needs to be approached with conscious reverence. Yet it is not something airy and remote, an act of piety disconnected from the real world. On the contrary, the holy supper points us directly into the real world. "The high point of our worship,'' Robert McAfee Brown once wrote, ''is not something ethereal—beautiful music, a pulpit voice, a lovely window. The high point is eating and drinking—the bread that intrudes from outside and represents Christ's body also represents sowing, and harvesting, and baking ovens, and teamsters' unions, and economics and politics, and those who have no bread, and all the rest'' (''True and False Witness,'' *Theology Today* 23, no. 4 [January 1967]: 527). To take that meal is not to participate in some self-serving ritual. It is to be given nourishment for the journey out into the world's life and to be joined to Christ in the building of his kingdom of peace and justice, world without end.

Good Friday

Lutheran	Roman Catholic	Episcopal	Pres/UCC/Chr	Meth/COCU
Isa. 52:13—53:12 or Hos. 6:1-6	Isa. 52:13—53:12	Isa. 52:13—53:12 or Gen. 22:1-18 or Wisd. 2:1, 12-24	Hos. 6:1-6	Isa. 52:13—53:12
Heb. 4:14-16; 5:7-9	Heb. 4:14-16; 5:7-9	Heb. 10:1-25	Rev. 5:6-14	Heb. 4:14-16; 5:7-9 or Heb. 10:1-25
John 18:1—19:42 or John 19:17-30	John 18:1—19:42	John (18:1-40) 19:1-37	Matt. 27:31-50	John 18:1—19:42 or Matt. 27:31-50

EXEGESIS

The Good Friday lessons are of course concerned to interpret the death of Jesus on the cross for Christians. The first two lessons show the inability of OT worship to bring people into a definitive and perfect relationship to God. The Gospel lesson shows Jesus as the trusting innocent person of the lament psalms, accepting all and leaving his vindication to God. It then goes farther and states that the sacrifice of Jesus as Son of God is efficacious for us all.

First Lesson: Hos. 6:1–6. Hosea exercised his prophetic ministry in the northern kingdom of Israel during its last troubled decades from about 755–724 B.C. The Neo-Assyrian Empire unrelentingly attacked during this time and reduced Israel's territory before capturing its capital city Samaria in 722 B.C. Internally the beleaguered kingdom suffered from dynastic instability and civil unrest. The events which gave rise to Hosea's portrayal of this moving dialogue between the people and their God cannot be known precisely, but one may conjecture that the kerygmatic unit 5:8—7:16 reflects the crises of 733 B.C. when the Assyrian king Tiglath-pileser III subdued the northern part of the kingdom and Pekah the Israelite king was murdered to be replaced by the pro-Assyrian Hoshea.

National distress was always an occasion for the people to call upon Yahweh the God of their nation for healing (vv. 1–3). In the light of the divine rebuke to their words in vv. 4–6, their prayer of vv. 1–3 must be interpreted as facile and presumptuous. Not bothering to express the sin which has led to the crisis, nor their repentance, the people through their priests make easy use of sacred language to express the expectation that Yahweh will automatically save. Vv. 1–2 have been variously understood by scholars, but the most likely interpretation is that they appeal to the divine healer to heal the sick nation (cf. Isa. 1:2–9). The Hebrew poetic device of parallelism is an important clue. "After two days" and "on the third day" are parallel phrases meaning a short time. The pair "revive" and "raise up" does not refer to resurrection. Attested in medical texts in the cognate languages and in Hebrew, the words mean simply to heal, to put the sick person back on his feet. The terms are used metaphorically in this passage of Yahweh healing the sick nation and returning it to normal within a very short time.

Mindless confidence that the Lord will always come is not true faith. True faith in God implies conversion to his ways (cf. Isa. 55:6–11). For this reason Yahweh rebukes his people with the exasperated questions of v. 4. The latter part of v. 4, "Your love is like a morning cloud," seems to mock the easy assurance of the people's prayer in v. 3b. Yahweh declares that his prophets' harsh words in the past have tried to instill in the people a love and fidelity in response to his own. He desires of his people not sacrifice and prayers alone but also steadfast love (*ḥesed*) and "knowledge of God," that is, loyal relationship. So in their hour of national crisis, the people are rebuked for their inadequate sacrifice because it is not sufficiently sincere and does not express the unconditional love and loyalty that Yahweh seeks. A Christian perspective suggests that God's desire for his people's love and loyalty is not satisfied with correct performance of ritual. With the critique of the worship the way is open for God to enable his people to respond to him in a more committed manner.

Second Lesson: Heb. 10:1-25. On Hebrews see Monday. Hebrews takes up the Hosean theme of OT sacrifice and its inability to bring about that union with God now offered to the Christian in Jesus. Heb. 8:1—10:31 is concerned with the sacrifice in the heavenly tabernacle, which is contrasted with sacrifice in the desert tabernacle described in Exodus, Leviticus, and Numbers. On the annual Day of Atonement under the old covenant (Leviticus 16), the high priest entered the Holy of Holies to make expiation for sin; and he entered with the blood of animals. Heb. 10:1-4 states that the OT ritual law is only a foreshadowing (*skia*) of the true form (*eikōn*), the effective reality. That the OT expiatory sacrifices must be repeated year after year is proof to the author that they are not the definitive reality. He concludes that the blood of bulls and goats is not able to take away sin once for all and to justify the believer before God (v. 4).

The author states his view of the ineffectiveness of OT sacrifice only to highlight the power of Christ's self-offering. He does this by bold reinterpretation of three Scripture passages, Psalms 40 and 110 and Jer. 31:31-34. Ps. 40:6-8a is attributed to Christ at his incarnation. Most Greek manuscripts have "but a body you have prepared for me" for the Hebrew text "an open ear you have prepared for me." The author adopts the Greek version since it supports his thesis that Jesus' sacrifice is the free offering of his own body. Jesus' offering of his bodily self has replaced the animal sacrifice of the old law. The Hebrew idiom of the first quoted verse of the psalm, "Sacrifices and offerings you have not desired," does not properly signify repudiation of ritual but only a preference for obedience. The author however interprets it as rejection of the OT sacrificial system in favor of the voluntary self-offering of Jesus. Psalm 110, originally a song for the installation of the Davidic king as king and priest on Mount Zion, had come to be used of the Messiah. The author expects the reader to be familiar with the whole psalm, which speaks of the king as a priest (Ps. 110:4). He is interested particularly in one detail—that the Anointed One is to sit at God's right hand. The Messiah's sitting is contrasted with the standing of the priests of the old law at daily service. They must repeatedly offer while Christ sits at the right hand of God, a gesture that shows his offering is fully accepted and need never be repeated. Sin is forgiven, which is the author's way of stating that we now have access to God in a way that we never did before. Jer. 31:33–34 is then cited so that one phrase can be highlighted: "I will remember their sins and their misdeeds no more."

The exhortation, vv. 19–25, using liturgical language (enter the sanctuary, curtain, flesh, draw near, great high priest over the house of God, hearts sprinkled clean, etc.) assures the reader of definitive access to God by reason of the once-for-all forgiveness of sin and urges all to assemble together in confidence that God is present to the congregation.

Hebrews is a Christian attempt to interpret the death of Christ against the background of OT sacrifice. Christ's death is so far superior to the death of animals in the OT system that it wipes it out and assures access once for all into God's presence.

Gospel: Matt. 27:31–50. The passage is an attempt to interpret the death of Jesus (which is the intention of Hebrews also) by giving a narrative account of it. The interpretation is done mainly through implicit or explicit quotations of certain psalms of lament from the OT Psalter, thus showing the death of Christ is in accord with the Scriptures. The lament psalms are the expressions of the just person persecuted by sinners who cries out to God for rescue and vindication. The psalmist portrays his or her case in stereotyped language as extreme—one is bereft of friends, overwhelmed by superior forces, publicly shamed and humiliated—so that the God of justice and of care for the poor will be moved to help in the hour of need. The drama has three actors: the sufferer, the wicked, and the God of justice and compassion. Essential to the OT genre is the expression of trust, even though sometimes it is only dimly present. The OT psalmist's prayer for public punishment of his or her enemies is really a prayer that God's justice be made visible so that people will see the justice of the psalmist's case. In the NT the resurrection functions as the public vindication of the unjustly persecuted Jesus. In Matt. 27:51–54, the rending of the temple curtain and the resurrection of the saints are divine vindications and function in the same way as the centurion's cry—to show publicly that Jesus was indeed a just man unjustly persecuted and that his enemies are sinners.

Matthew and the fixed tradition of the passion upon which he depends set the account of the crucifixion within the lament psalm tradition. The "myrrhed wine" of v. 34 seems to allude to the Greek text of Ps. 69:21, "They gave me also gall for my food, and made me drink vinegar for my thirst"; also v. 48 to Ps. 69:20, where the psalmist finds no understanding friend in distress. The dividing of Jesus' garments takes up Ps. 22:18, a psalm of lament again alluded to in the derision of the passersby (v. 39 and Ps. 22:7), in the sarcastic reference to the sufferer's trust in God in time of distress (v. 43 and Ps. 22:8), and finally in the cry upon the cross (v. 46 and Ps. 22:1). His death with robbers appears to refer to the fourth servant song in Isa. 53:12. The framework of quotations establishes Jesus as the suffering just person of the OT, for whom suffering and humiliation are not a sign of God's rejection but a prelude to rescue and judgment of the sinners who persecuted him.

The evangelist interprets the death as a divinely willed event that was accepted by Jesus in trust of ultimate rescue and vindication. In so doing he shows the same concern as the author of Hebrews, though with different use of the OT, to portray the shocking event as meaningful for his readers.

God has accepted the voluntary self-offering of Jesus just as he accepted the OT just persons' entrusting of their lives to him in the lament psalms. But because Jesus is truly the King of Israel (v. 42) and the Son of God (v. 43), his offering is on a different scale than that of the heroes of old. This sacrifice is indeed efficacious, bringing the people before God in a perfectly acceptable manner.

HOMILETICAL INTERPRETATION

We come to God's Friday, to the end of Holy Week. On this day the preacher is charged by the Scripture to illuminate God's purposes as they are revealed in suffering and death, even the suffering and death of the Messiah. It is no easy assignment. Yet because the preacher is also pastor, week by week facing suffering and death in human life, the task of wrestling with the cosmic ambiguity of Good Friday can have a kind of domestic familiarity in it. It is a day we have met very many times since the last Holy Week: it is the day when a doctor speaks the dread word "malignant" to a young mother and she asks the inevitable "Why me?"; the day when a drunken driver, rushing mindlessly past a red light, crushes a child's life, leaving a family in stricken bewilderment; it is the day when hopelessness triumphs in a man's heart and he throws himself out a window, scattering guilt and remorse upon all who knew him and loved him. We know this day well. We have now only to find its goodness.

First Lesson: Hos. 6:1–6. The first of the day's lessons comes from the prophetic book attributed to one Hosea, whose name, the commentators say, is derived from the Hebrew word "to deliver." According to the biographical parts of the book, Hosea's own deliverance was into a life of humiliation and sorrow, the primary cause for which was the persistent unfaithfulness of his wife. In spite of his grief, Hosea's extraordinary response to her betrayals was an equally persistent love; in his love we are given a figure of God's unremitting love for Israel.

The prophecy that is associated with Hosea has very much to do, then, with the steadfast love of God. It is a love which prevails, a love which is present in the days of Israel's ruination as much as in days of triumph. It is a love which is indifferent to indifference, willing to keep faith even with a faithless and presumptuous people. "Come, let us return to the Lord," they say (v. 1) in the halfhearted singsong voices of the conventionally pious. Yet the love persists, tracking them down in loving judgment.

The response that love seeks is not in the carrying out of the little dramas of conventional religion. It is in that activity of persistent selflessness which is itself love.

In the middle of Paddy Chayefsky's play *Gideon,* the angel of the Lord and Gideon are in conversation and the angel laments, "I have loved you [Gideon], and you have turned your back." Gideon: "I do find you personable, sir." The Angel: "Personable! Gideon, one does not merely fancy God. I demand a splendid love from you, abandoned adoration, a torrent, a storm of love" ([New York: Random House, 1961] p. 54).

Let the first word on this Good Friday be of the extravagant love of God, the love that persists through every pain and every outrage of the human spirit, the love that calls forth loving.

Second Lesson: Heb. 10:1-25. As though to keep before us the primary contentions of our faith, the lectionary returns us in this Second Lesson to the Letter to the Hebrews. In its intricate analogies and its scholarly references to Scripture and tradition we are confronted again with the meaning of Christ's willingness to die. In a way, what it says is that Good Friday is also Necessary Friday, the day on which God acts to free men and women from the prisons of their own making. It is, the author claims, the only way that kind of freedom could be had. By what happens in Christ on this dark day our worth is secured. Not by obedience to our laws, not by the solemnity of our rituals, but by the death of Christ we are rendered so worthy that we are free even to defy the commandments of God and reject his precious Son.

There is very much in our practice of religion that simply does not acknowledge those claims at all. So far from rejoicing in the free gift from God which is our freedom, we are inclined to make our occasions for worship into times dominated by guilty remorse. In place of the lightheartedness that ought to follow from liberation, we are moved to chant of our culpability and our sorrow.

Worship on Good Friday may lend itself especially to this murky, unbiblical tendency in us. Too much time may be spent identifying the "murderers of Jesus," pointing out the people who ought to bear the blame—perhaps feeling all along that we are just those guilty ones. There *is* a sense in which the dread responsibility for the crucifixion rests upon us all, even a sense in which we continue to wield hammers and nails against him by the cruelties we permit in our lives. Nothing in this fragment of the Letter to the Hebrews, or anywhere in the NT, denies those things. They are acknowledged; and then it is claimed that the cross of Christ has canceled them all—every cruelty, every act of lovelessness and indifference, every sample of our sinfulness.

Somehow, the preacher needs to try to let the power of that astonishing claim into Good Friday's worship. The sobriety in what we do in our liturgy on this day ought to come from awe and not from guilt. Awe because, as the writer of this letter says in another place, "Christ has not entered into the holy places made with hands, which are the figures of the true; but into heaven itself, now to appear in the presence of God for us" (Heb. 9:24). For us. Let it be heard that this day, above all days, is for us.

Gospel: Matt. 27:31–50. Now we are made to hear the story. In this lectionary it is set forth in Matthew's stylized version, replete with echoes of Hebraic faith. (See exegesis.) Yet even in this account there is an unmistakable feeling of the commonplace. There is something despairingly *ordinary* about the scenes: the brutality of men picking on one of their own kind (the bullies in this case happen to be soldiers—a fact that sharpens the cruelty by giving it the stamp of official authority); the matter-of-fact little death march to the usual place for executions; the sadistic delight of hangers-on and passersby. It all seems so commonplace. Even the irate keepers of the tradition and the insecure and testy politicians who brought the whole matter to a head—even they appear as stock characters, verifiable in familiar human experience.

There is something to hear in the very ordinariness of the savagery of that day. It is that in his death as in his life, Christ took upon himself all the ordinariness of our days. Of course there is drama here. Knowing who he is, we hear of his trial and execution, and our hearts leap in apprehension and despair. But the drama is made up of familiar things, things that come to hand in every human life: venial pride, casual brutality, the reflex for vengeance, the fear of the truth. They are the customary flaws in us, and as they are unleashed upon the just sufferer we are reminded again of the banality of evil. That is surely one word to us at the end of our

Holy Week: that the assault upon the goodness of God is made from the barricades of the ordinary.

There is another word, however, and it too arises out of the ordinary. Perhaps it is best expressed in the figure of Simon, the man of Cyrene, who is said to have carried the crossbar of the weakening victim. He had the commonest of names for his place and time. There is no evidence in any account to suggest that there was anything at all unusual about him. By a happenstance he is swept up into the world's cataclysm and given the work of relieving Jesus.

There is something telling in that, something certainly true about the Christian life: that we can relieve Jesus; that ordinary workaday human beings are capable of affecting the life of God. What God says in the little vignette of unremarkable Simon, carrying the cross of the anointed King of heaven and earth, is that God's life and human life are forevermore of a piece. Not only does the life of God, by merciful love and extravagant pity, affect us, nourishing our hearts and mending our poor spirits. By our acts of love and mercy *we* can affect the life of God. Surely that is what Jesus meant when he told his followers that when they gave refreshment to the suffering least of all their brothers and sisters, *he* was refreshed, *he* given relief, *he* unburdened.

The last Good Friday word is, then, of hope. It is hope born of the shimmering truth that in the death of Christ every ordinary one of us is offered the possibility of life, that in the seeming pointlessness of his crucifixion our lives are given purpose and meaning.

Holy Week and the Holy Task

A Note to Preachers

In the midst of that sublime discourse from the seventeenth century which is George Herbert's treatise on the high vocation of the country parson, there are some cautionary words for the preacher. Ever the practical counselor, Herbert speaks in particular. The sermon, he says, ought not to be longer than an hour! It ought to include appropriate, instructive illustrations with which the congregation can readily identify. It ought to avoid generalities. And so on. Then, at the heart of his counsel, he breaks off from practical advice. "Sermons are dangerous things," he says, since "none goes out of Church as he came in, but either better or worse." As though that were not a sufficiently intimidating observation for the reader who has regular appointments to keep in a pulpit, Herbert goes on to say that the *real* character of the sermon does not depend upon techniques at all, but upon holiness. The preacher, he says, is not called to be "witty, or learned, or eloquent, but Holy." In those words from a gentle poet, who said of himself and his calling that he was a "domestic servant to the King of Heaven," there is revealed both the burden of preaching and its glory. Never are those things felt more acutely than in Holy Week.

The precarious task of the Holy Week preacher begins, as it does for the preacher in any week, with words from ancient sources. The first work is to draw close to those sources, to gain whatever sense can be gained about the things that really informed and shaped them. The biblical story is distant, if time and culture are the measures, but for the preacher it must never be remote. If the Holy Week accounts are to be truly contemporary, such that they touch and move contemporary lives, the proclamation of their meaning has to have its roots in the ancient landscape upon which those accounts were born.

Of course this is a work more easily commended than accomplished. In one sense we cannot jump out of late twentieth-century skins and adopt the perspective of, say, an exiled prophet of the fractured Israel of the sixth century B.C., or see the events of God's saving history with the eyes of a citizen of Rome and member of the koinonia of the infant church. Still, the preacher needs to reach for those perspectives, to ask of the text from whence it came and why, to hear what can be heard of the original claims it makes upon the people of God.

Although it is no easy undertaking, there are allies on every hand: translators and lexicographers and commentators of several kinds. If their lights can be combined with even a modest knowledge of the biblical languages, the first step toward proclamation is achieved. It is the step of study, of course, the step of scholarship; but because it is not scholarship for its own sake it can have a different life from that of most study. There is a point of contact with the life of prayer when the preacher is studious about the biblical texts. It is a work to be undertaken with a determination to uncover the purposes of God, in just the way that contemplative prayer is undertaken. When that happens, though the going may be hard, it is never heavy with the dreary weights of pedantry.

The lectionary we are given for this Holy Week combines prophetic vision and teaching about Christian doctrine and the narrative of the Passion. Each of those elements needs to be discovered in terms of its own origins, each needs to be probed by the delicate instruments of human learning. Each needs to be approached as a part of the ongoing intentions of the God who shows his hand in human history.

Above everything, this week is dominated by the story of the passion of Christ. *Passion* is a curiously double-edged English word. If one reads it in the morning paper, it almost certainly refers to behavior marked by sharp initiative and dramatic action of some kind. The passionate political reformer is the one who storms the gates of social indifference; the passionate operagoer, the one who stands all night outside a ticket window for the sake of a single seat for a performance of *Parsifal;* the passionate lover, the person who acts with reckless impulse toward the object of his passion. Yet in its ancient roots the word *passion,* like the word *patient*—which shares those roots—refers to suffering. The Holy Week preacher needs, perhaps, to acknowledge that this week is about passion in both those meanings. It is about the way in which our stormy and driven lives are met by the sublime acceptance of the suffering God.

To speak the truth about that meeting is the task of the preacher during the days of this darkest, holiest week. To do it so that the proclamation has meaning now, in the bewildering present, requires the asking of some sharp questions—about ourselves and our origins as well as about the origins of the Scripture over which we pore. What is it that most affects *us* as we try to come to terms with the holy story? What is it that blurs our vision, or sharpens it, as we gaze upon the sacred events that are at the heart of the Christian life? What influences of race and sex and class and social and economic reality bear upon us as we seek to discover the meaning of God's passionate love in our days? To ask questions of that kind is to embark upon the difficult, necessary journey into our own history, a history as thoroughly charged with the plans and the purposes of God as is any distant day. Preachers cannot escape the conditions of the history in which they find themselves, but neither should they be so implicated in those conditions that they reduce the great biblical claims to the puny dimensions of some modern ideology. The gospel's truth is spoken through human institutions and human systems, but it is never contained by them. If preachers are to be the vehicles of that truth, they must be willing, ultimately, to abandon even the dearest of their ideological convictions in the face of the biblical claim upon them.

The form that the biblical claim takes in Holy Week arises out of the gentle assertion that God joins us in our suffering. It is astonishing news: that our suffering—the suffering of a war-threatened, poverty-ridden planet, the suffering that has taken up residence in the lives of the people in the pews all around us—all of that is met and touched and shared by the suffering God. To be able truly to make that claim requires of the preacher an openness to the world's pain. It requires a sensitivity to the devastation of human life which is the bitter fruit of economic injustice; it requires an awareness of the crippling of the human spirit by the brutal forces of totalitarian governments; it requires a susceptibility to the human misery which lies in dread potential in the world's armament depots. And the preacher's openness to the pain of the world also requires that he or she speak out against it, calling it by its proper name, summoning the people of God to war against it by the works of justice and mercy and healing. When the Lord of history took the world's pain into his own body he did not receive it without complaint, but cried out against it in anguish. In the week in which we particularly remember his cries, the preacher dare not keep silent about the outrage of the suffering of the world's life.

Some of the world's suffering is shared between preacher and people in deep and intimate ways, and that sharing is bound to be part of the Holy Week proclamation. For the preacher is also the pastor, the one who is charged with the terrifying privilege of joining in the agony of others. Every sermon is surely touched by that experience, but perhaps in this week of passion the preaching is marked more deeply than ever by the experience of preacher and people of the suffering they have shared. By the preaching of the Word, the preacher can be the emblem and focal point for the great yearnings of grief and despair which shake the hearts of the gathered company of the people of God. By that same Word can come also the restorative assurance that no one is ever alone in his suffering, that there is no misery so great, no pain so sharp, that God does not join us in it. In that curious meeting of sorrow and comfort there is great wonder for the preacher, and the beauty of holiness.

HAYS H. ROCKWELL